CONRAD the MAN,
the WRITER, the POLE

To my wife

By the same Author:

Wstęp do Lorda Jima. (Introduction to *Lord Jim*), 1946.
Conrad żywy (The Living Conrad) with an English Summary, 1957.
Ucieczka (The Escape). A volume of short stories, 1960.
Ucieczka (2nd revised edition), 1982.
Mój ojciec (My father), biography, 1966.
Conrad człowiek, pisarz, Polak (Conrad the Man, the Writer, the Pole), 1972.
Wyznania i aforyzmy (Confessions and aphorisms), 1974.
Ksiądz Antoni (Father Anthony). A novel, 1977.
Pisarze chrześcijańskiej rozpaczy (The Writers of Christian Despair: Graham Greene, François Mauriac, Georges Bernanos), 1977.
Od Gombrowicza do Mackiewicza (Gombrowicz and Other Writers), 1980.
Opowieści o niebie i ziemi (Tales of Heaven and Earth), 1979.

Translations from Conrad

Under Western Eyes, 1974
The Sisters, 1974.
"Prince Roman", 1975.

£1·50

WIT M. TARNAWSKI

CONRAD the MAN, the WRITER, the POLE

An Essay in Psychological Biography

Translated by Rosamond Batchelor

POLISH CULTURAL FOUNDATION

London 1984

Published by Polish Cultural Foundation Limited,
9 Charleville Road, London W14 9JL.

ISBN 0 85065 125 5

Cover design:
Grzegorz Sowula

Printed in Great Britain by Caldra House Ltd.
23 Coleridge Street, Hove, Sussex BN3 5AB.

CONTENTS

PART IV

THE AGEING CONRAD

INSTEAD OF A FOREWARD
by John Conrad

The Howe,
Vicarage Hill,
Petham.

16th April 1980

Dear Wit,

Now that I have read your book I am amazed at your perception of my father through his books—your understanding of J.C. is so profound and sensible that others who have written about him, with several notable exceptions, appear to be almost lacking in any deep insight; but then, they are not Polish, though that detracts nothing from your achievement.

It was a strong temptation to read your book through when I first received it, but I refrained, as I was in the throes of getting my own book ready for printing, and I was afraid that I should be tempted to alter my book after reading yours. I need not have worried, as the books seem to me to complement one another—your book provides the other half to my recollections, that part of J.C's life which was not shared with the family.

With all our best wishes and sincere affection,

Yours,

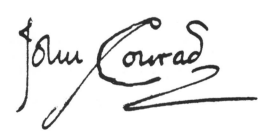

AUTHOR'S PREFACE

"Conrad the Man, the Writer, the Pole": the title gives, I think, a good idea of the theme of my book. It is, more precisely, an attempt to show how the man, as an individual, and the Pole, as heir to a distinctive cultural tradition, both play a vital part in the writer. Conrad was an author whose works all bear the strong imprint of his personality. As he himself said, "a novelist lives in his work. He stands there, the only reality in an invented world, among imaginary things, happenings, and people. Writing about them, he is only writing about himself."* To discover the personality behind the work is always an absorbing task, but in the case of Conrad it has a fascination of its own.

Although modern criticism does not approve of this method, and tries to keep the author and his work apart, we find, in studying Conrad's writings, that the results of a comparative analysis are too valuable to be sacrificed for the sake of a modern trend. The work and the writer continually throw light on each other, and by separating them we lessen our understanding of both. Moreover, Conrad's inner life reveals depths no less fascinating than those found in his works.

There is, however, one danger in the approach I have chosen. Any attempt to construct Conrad's biography from the material provided by his books calls for a good deal of guess-work; and a guess may be right or wrong. But every science owes its progress to hypotheses; without them there would be no discoveries and no new realms of knowledge.

The studies which make up this book are the work of many years. When I decided to publish them in book-form, I had to choose between two alternatives. I could either try to give an inner portrait of Conrad, in all its diversity, or I could confine myself to some of his major themes and preoccupations, and trace their interplay and development.

There were two reasons for my deciding on the second course: it seemed more likely to result in a clear presentation, and to provide better opportunities for bringing essential matters to the fore. It had also the merit of introducing Conrad's problems in a more systematic way than would have been possible had I attempted to discuss the rich and complex totality.

---

*"A Familiar Preface" to *A Personal Record*, p. XIII.

From the time when Conrad embarked on a literary career, two major concerns dominated his life and writing:

(1) The problem of his relationship to his native country, seen in connection with the charge of desertion brought against him in Poland—a charge with which, for the rest of his life, he struggled to come to terms.

(2) His impassioned criticism of the materialistic civilisation of the West, which inspired two of his greatest works—"Heart of Darkness" and *Nostromo*.

Most of the essays in this book are devoted to an examination of one or other of these two pivotal themes. A third group of essays, linking the other two, discusses his Russian novel, *Under Western Eyes*, in which national and personal preoccupations merge with international problems as yet another version of the motif of betrayal, and an attempt to form a final judgment on the opposed civilisations of East and West.

I hope that my book achieves structural unity through its consistent purpose in probing into the mind and problems of Conrad, the man and the writer.

The book was first published in Polish in London in 1972. In preparing the English edition, I had virtually to re-write it, by cutting out chapters that would be of no interest to English readers, and adding material. I also re-grouped the contents of the book and revised the whole text, changing a great deal. The book I now present to English readers is in fact a completely new version of the former text.

ACKNOWLEDGEMENTS

I should like to express my sincere gratitude to all those who have contributed to the making of my book.

In particular I am greatly indebted to John Conrad, who, to my sorrow, did not live to see its publication; to Rosamond Batchelor for her devoted work over the translation; to Mrs. Juliet McLauchlan Chairman of the Joseph Conrad Society (U.K.) for her continuous support and numerous kindnesses; to Professor Norman Sherry of the University of Lancaster and Professor Ian Watt of Stanford University, California, for their most helpful advice regarding the contents and structure of the book; to Eloise Knapp Hay, author of *The Political Novels of Joseph Conrad,* who kindly agreed to my including the exchange of letters with her on the subject of Conrad's guilt-complex; to John Crompton, the former editor of the Journal of the Joseph Conrad Society (U.K.) for his instructive commentary on the contents of my book; to my nephew, Andrzej Busza, Professor of the University of British Columbia, for preparing the index and footnotes; and finally to Mrs. Ewa Czaykowska-Higgins for helping me with the proof-reading of the text; and to all my English and Polish friends who have given me help and encouragement. I am also grateful to the Beinecke Rare Book and Manuscript Library, Yale University, for permission to reproduce photographs in its possession.

W. T.

PART I

CONRAD, THE MAN AND THE WRITER

THE MIRROR OF CONRAD

Conrad was undoubtedly frank by nature; he longed to communicate with others and to share with them his own deeply felt truth. It is significant how often he quotes the words of Novalis: "My conviction gains infinitely the moment another soul will believe in it."*

Yet, the apparently spontaneous declarations that one finds in his numerous forewords, or even in *A Personal Record,* often give the impression that he is scattering fragments of the truth in order to conceal its essence. If one tries, from his own statements, to form a clear idea of his beliefs and feelings, one soon comes up against contradictions and loses one's way. Even a study of the biographical material, of which there is now so much, does not lead one out of the labyrinth. Conrad's letters, and his remarks in private conversation, are sometimes direct and strongly expressed, at other times evasive and clearly intended to throw one off the scent; they are no less contradictory than his public utterances. Sooner or later, the student of Conrad has to ask himself: Did this man, fundamentally so honest, and at times so startlingly outspoken, always speak the truth? To answer this question, one must ask another: Would the frankest and most straightforward man remain frank and straightforward if he were in Conrad's position? Anyone who is familiar with Conrad's life and works knows that he was dogged by a lifelong sense of guilt—the guilt of having left his country, deserted his post. He himself wrote in his *Personal Record:* "It would take too long to explain the intimate alliance of contradictions in human nature which makes love itself wear at times the desperate shape of betrayal." A man who is incessantly haunted by this sense of guilt can neither be consistent and simple

---

*Motto to *Lord Jim.*

in his reactions nor altogether sincere in what he says and writes; there is always something that he has to hide; always something to explain away. The more honest he is, and the more sensitive his conscience, the more moody and reserved he will be. Only a cynic has no great difficulty in laying bare his flaws—which cause him no particular concern.

Quite apart from this, however, and even had there been no interior drama to complicate Conrad's outward behaviour, it would not have been easy for him to be completely frank in his relations with others. Isolated as he was by his Polish and aristocratic origins from the international crowd around him, he inevitably felt himself to be different, alien and baffling. It gradually became second nature to him to hide the truth about himself, and to practise the inevitable evasions.

Conrad was, of course, too great, he had risen too far above the human average not to have been, to some extent, "alone among men", even had he never left his native country. But his loneliness and reserve would then have been of a different order. Nothing is harder than to be frank and open when one is among strangers, surrounded by people to whom many things in one's life are incomprehensible—people whose attitude to foreigners is often suspicious or hostile, and in whose company, if one does not want to be regarded as an outsider, one has always to wear a mask.

Even this, however, was not all. The frequent changes and inconsistencies in Conrad's writings and talk were not entirely due to the fact that he was in a foreign country, and burdened with a sense of guilt. His own temperament counted for much. He was by nature extremely emotional and changeable, subject to continual waves of depression and elation, pessimism and sudden hope. These emotional variations were intensified by his far-ranging and perceptive intelligence, which saw everything from different angles. To men like him, the world is apt to appear alternately black or white, and their own conduct either irreproachable or full of mistakes and shortcomings. Everything changes its aspect according to the mood of the moment, and they are able, with perfect sincerity, to express opinions that are in flat contradiction to each other.

This, of course, explains why, however equivocal he may be, the note of sincerity is never lacking in Conrad. The literature of the world does not contain many writers in whom, beneath the shifting tides of their moods, one can find so solid a bedrock of character, or feel such strong currents of emotion sweeping along the same channels and returning to the same problems. Despite this, it is not always easy to discover Conrad's essential consistency under his changeability, or to see what lay behind his often contradictory statements.

Fortunately, Conrad was a writer. It is possible to say of him, with more truth than of most, that he wrote because he had to write. Writing was the only way he had of speaking out, of sharing his inner truth with others, of "showing his wounds to the crowd". The confessions in a work of art are anonymous, defying all identification and control—sometimes even the control of the author himself, who feels there hidden and completely safe. In the disguise of symbols and imaginary characters and events, he can express himself fearlessly and unreservedly—his whole self, with all his dreams, anxieties, and conflicts.

Conrad's works, then, however impersonal and objective they may appear, are permeated by subjectivity, and it is to them that we must look for the undisguised and ultimate truth about him. A perceptive eye and a sensitive ear will always find his books a storehouse of revealing information about the author; they point unerringly to the inner truth among the conflicting opinions of biographers and the disputable statements of the author himself.

In the '50s, there appeared a book entitled *The Mirror of Conrad,* whose author, E. H. Visiak, tried to build up Conrad's life-story from events and formulations contained in his work. The book itself is somewhat superficial, and too literal in its interpretation of the material in the novels. But the title was a good one. The fiction of the author of *The Mirror of the Sea* is the truest and most complete mirror of Conrad.

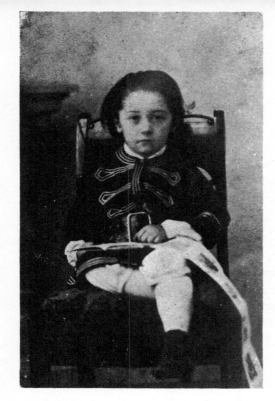

The five-year-old
Conrad in
exile in Vologda.

The dedication that appears
on the back of the above
photograph. "To my dear
Granny who helped me to
send cakes to my poor Daddy
in prison.
Grandson, Pole, Catholic
and Gentleman.
Konrad".

10

THE GENESIS OF A WRITER

1

What made Conrad start writing? Why did he, a sailor, after many years at sea, suddenly become a writer, although, as he tells us, he had never before written a line? (A statement that we can take with a grain of salt.)

The answer is simple: it happened because it had to happen: sooner or later, Conrad was bound to write. It is rather as though one asked why people fall in love when they are young. Where there is a pile of inflammable material, any spark will set it off; it is just a matter of chance or coincidence when the stray spark alights on the powder.

Everything in Conrad's life predestined him to be a writer; his whole childhood was a preparation for it. I do not mention, as a *conditio sine qua non,* his innate and powerful creative gift, or the profound and sensitive personality which nurtured it. That, however, was not all; as a poet's son, he had, from his earliest years, imbibed his literary standards and love of books from his father. Conrad, as a boy, was already writing historical plays; and, when a cousin asked him what he wanted to be, he replied, "A great writer".

There were many other things that fanned his inborn talent into flame. There was his isolation among uneducated and alien people, with whom he had almost nothing in common. There was the gradual accumulation of new experience and observations, all seeking expression. There were newly arisen conflicts and complexes—the sense of disloyalty to his country, of disillusionment with the country for which he had left it, and of increasing melancholy. Even had he been willing to speak of these things, he could never have done so. His only possible outlet was writing—writing about other people, as a way of writing about himself.

The question still remains: why did Conrad begin so late? Had he stayed in his own country, he would probably have started writing much earlier—first poetry, as is usually the way, and then prose. The main reason for his late start is surely the time it took him to master the tool of his craft—the foreign language in which he was to write. His love of adventure and passion for seeing the world were also factors making for delay. Moreover, his earlier impressions were so deeply overlaid by the richness and diversity of his later experiences that he found it difficult to combine them creatively. But, I repeat, what most held him up was the indispensable period of his apprenticeship to the English language—the only language, as he himself said, in which he could write, and certainly the one which best lent itself to recording his experiences as a sailor and traveller in exotic countries.

Here, however, we are faced by a still more baffling question. Why did Conrad, homeless wanderer though he was, never try to write about this new material in his own language? His uncle Bobrowski had urged him to send accounts of his travels to Polish periodicals, and would no doubt have arranged matters for him. Even here, the answer is probably simpler and more comprehensible than it seems at first. We must remember Conrad's early uprooting from his native soil, and the fact that for twenty years he was completely cut off from readers in Poland, whose very existence must have seemed almost unreal to him. Again, his knowledge of his own language may have grown rusty; in any case, Polish had, at that time, almost no nautical terminology, and would have been ill-fitted to describe life at sea. And who can guess all the other factors that made Conrad postpone the expression of his new being until he had acquired complete mastery over his tool—the language of his future creative work? But when he had mastered it, any spark was enough to start the blaze—and it mattered little what that spark was.

We have, indeed, in *A Personal Record,* the author's official statement concerning the matter—an exact account of how *Almayer's Folly* came to be written. We now know, of course, that this statement does not tell the whole truth. Three years before he wrote *Almayer's Folly,* Conrad had submitted his first story, "The Black Mate", to a literary competition in *Tit-Bits*. His assertion that

Almayer was his first literary attempt may be taken to mean, at most, that it marked the beginning of his serious and, by now, mature creative work. All this, however, is of no great importance. One way or another, Conrad would have started writing as soon as he felt capable of handling and expressing himself freely in the language of his choice.

The Joseph Conrad bibliography compiled by K. A. Lohf and E. P. Sheehy and published in 1957 ran to 114 pages and contained 1,256 items. The next bibliography (1971), that of B. E. Teets and H. E. Gerber, had 670 pages and 1971 selected entries. This is surely a sign of the growing interest in Conrad during the intervening years. But in spite of this interest, relatively little is known of the most fascinating, and, it may be added, the decisive period of his life—the years between 1887 and 1894, when the writer was, quite unexpectedly, beginning to come to life in the sailor. Conrad's profuse correspondence, and the considerable amount of information supplied by his friends, goes back only to 1895—the year in which *Almayer's Folly* was published. Before this vital year, his life—apart from his correspondence with his uncle Bobrowski, of which only the Bobrowski letters have survived—is a blank page. Anything, therefore, that can make this period clearer to us is of great value. Two books, both published in 1966, throw light on this important period. Each does so from a different angle, but each, in its own way, admirably.

The first is a collection of letters from Conrad to Marguerite Poradowska, a French writer, related to him by marriage. The collection was published and edited by René Rapin, the late Professor of French literature at Lausanne University. The recipient of the letters had become Conrad's aunt by marrying his uncle, Alexander Poradowski. By the time the correspondence began, in 1890, his uncle Poradowski was dead, and, for the next few years, Conrad was obviously in love with his beautiful aunt. The great value of the letters lies, therefore, not only in their being the one fairly large collection of his writings before his life as an author began (his invaluable letters to his uncle Bobrowski disappeared in the Ukraine during the First World War), but also in the fact that the future writer, emotionally involved as he was, expressed himself with exceptional openness and spontaneity.

The period of Conrad's most frequent letters to his literary aunt more or less coincides with the time when he was writing *Almayer's Folly*. It is only by reading the letters to Madame

Poradowska that we begin to understand why the experienced sailor and fearless seeker after adventure, who was to create so many heroes of duty (as well as deserters from it), began his literary career by writing a drama of defeat and disillusionment: why, among the multitude of human types that he had encountered all over the world, it was Almayer, the failure and weakling, who fascinated the writer at the outset of his career.

Here are a few significant self-revelations taken at random from Conrad's letters to his aunt. On the 15th May 1890, he wrote, while on his way to the Congo: "A few illusions, many dreams, an occasional gleam of happiness, then disillusionment, some anger and much suffering, and, finally, the end—peace. Such is the programme, and we must play out the tragi-comedy to the end. One just has to put up with it." And, on the 12th June 1890, "For a long time I cared nothing where my path was taking me. I went along it with lowered head, cursing the stones."

This tendency to pessimism was, of course, increased by his grim experiences in the Congo, and by the malaria that he caught there. His letters between 1891 and 1895 are a series of similar bitter comments on life and himself. For instance: "One must go on to the end, since one has had the misfortune to be born"; or, "I feel that I have not seen anything, that I am not seeing anything, and that I shall never see anything. I could swear that, beyond the walls of this room, there lies only the void."

The link between Conrad and his hero Almayer is evident. In the figure of this hopeless outcast the existing moods and innermost fears of Conrad were embodied in their strongest form. This, then, was how the romantic quest for the beauty of life usually ended—with the slow decay of a human wreck in tropical heat.

It would take too long to examine all the reasons for so pessimistic an attitude. But to sum up in a few words what should be explained over several pages, one may say that Conrad had, by that time, crossed his "shadow line". The gleam of the adventures for whose sake he had set out from Poland for distant seas had flickered out and left him a disappointed man. The new, and real, purpose of his life—creative writing—had not yet seized hold of him; he was still groping after it. He was in a vacuum. And then Almayer came to him. "But if I had not got to know Almayer pretty well," he wrote later in *A Personal Record*, "it is almost certain there would never have been a line of mine in print."*

A Personal Record, p. 87.

The second book—*Conrad's Eastern World*, by Norman Sherry—is the exact opposite of the first. Where Conrad's letters to Madame Poradowska had laid bare, in an unusually intimate way, Conrad's moods and feelings at the time when he was writing *Almayer's Folly*, Sherry's book deals only with the external facts that had given the author his material for the plot of his first novel. The books complement each other, and put before us the two realities out of which the novel was born.

Sherry was in an exceptionally fortunate position for collecting his data. As lecturer in English at Singapore University, he had lived at the very centre of the territory which Conrad had visited on his Malayan voyages, some years before he wrote *Almayer's Folly*. With the tireless patience of a research worker and the penetration of a detective, Sherry gathered together every scrap of information about the great writer that could still be unearthed in that part of the world—information concerning the people he had known, the places he had visited, and the ships he had sailed in.

But Sherry's book did more than collect an enormous number of hitherto unknown facts concerning Conrad's Malayan past. His book has a deeper significance, for it gives us a fascinating insight into the psychology of creative art. Sherry shows us, as no previous Conrad scholar had done, and with an immense amount of new material to back his assertions, exactly how Conrad's creative imagination had worked to transform reality into art.

We learn from Sherry's book that there is hardly a character or event in Conrad's Malayan books that is not based on some aspect of the reality of life in Malaya. Even the names of people and ships were seldom invented; in nearly every case, Sherry discovered a corresponding original. As regards *Almayer's Folly*—a work of outstanding importance for a Conrad student as being the writer's first venture into literature—we find that not only Almayer himself but almost all the secondary characters in the novel were founded, to some extent, on real models, as was the description of local trading conditions, and of the settlement in which Almayer lived.

Sherry explains this close connection between Conrad's work and the known facts of his life by a lack of creative imagination in the author, whom he quotes as saying that he was "unable to invent anything".

We should not take Conrad too literally here. It is hard to accuse of a lack of imagination the man who, in *Nostromo*, created

15

the state of Costaguana on the strength of a few days' stay in Central America (he did, of course, deepen his knowledge by serious study of the history and geography of the area). Facts, to him, seem to have been little more than the spark that ignited his imagination. Moreover, he invariably breathed into figures based on reality the deeper and more complex souls that he himself had invented; and it is in these souls, and not in outward events, that we find the true essence of Conrad's art.

It was, then, something other than a lack of creative imagination that made him cling so tenaciously to concrete facts, and feel a need for solid ground beneath his feet. It seems to me that, besides the general law governing creativity—the law that every work of art is, to some extent, inspired by concrete facts—Conrad's work as a sailor played a part that should not be overlooked. His life at sea taught him to observe closely and to appreciate the importance of the most minute details in the surrounding reality, since the conscientious performance of his work, and sometimes his life itself, depended on his doing so. And this ingrained nautical habit was transferred to his art, when Captain Korzeniowski exchanged the mariner's telescope for the pen of a novelist.

SOME REMARKS ON CONRAD'S ART AND PERSONALITY

Conrad — a Figure of the Renaissance

The critics disagreed from the first as to how Conrad should be classified. Was he a writer of adventure stories, or a chronicler of the soul—a novelist obsessed by the exotic, or a moralist? Conrad himself was sometimes furious at being regarded as no more than a writer of the sea. Indeed, only a man of extremely limited vision would want to label Conrad at all. Yet the wish to fit people into categories is comprehensible. Specialisation in both art and science is characteristic of our day. Faced as we are with a vast and ever-increasing number of observable phenomena, we are forced to give up all hope of exploring these widening horizons, and to confine ourselves to some small and well-defined field. Much is gained by this specialisation, but something of great value is lost— the vision of the whole, and of the relation between the parts and the whole: and, without this vision, the parts often cannot be understood.

The same applies to modern fiction. Its various ramifications— the psychological novel, the adventure story, the "nouveau roman" and so on—are as far apart today as they ever were. We have to go back to Balzac and his contemporaries, or to the Russian novelists of the nineteenth century, to find examples of interlinking between the various kinds of fiction. In the work of contemporary novelists—those, of course, who count—we find none of this interconnection. Nearly all the writers of our day pursue their own narrow path in the art of fiction, and only very rarely change their course.

It would, however, be vain to look for any such distinct lines of demarcation in the work of Conrad. He was, of course, primarily interested in what goes on in a man's soul, but he was also fascinated by an exotic background or an exciting adventure. In the books of his first creative period, up to and including—let us say—*Under Western Eyes*—psychological themes prevail; the later books deal more and more with dramas of the emotions, or with stirring events, as though the experiences of youth exerted an even stronger fascination from a distance, at a time when all hope of discovering the full truth about man was beginning to fade. But throughout the whole of his literary career Conrad showed a masterly power of combining the adventurous elements in his novels with the psychological: plot with analysis.

Nor is this all. In a letter to an American publisher, William R. Kane,* who had asked Conrad to describe for the benefit of his "brethren of the pen", his own experiences as a writer, Conrad replied that he could only indicate a few general moral principles. I suspect that most of his "brethren of the pen" either failed to understand what he meant, or shrugged their shoulders contemptuously. Art and morality, to Conrad's contemporaries, had long since parted company. But all Conrad's books breathe a moral atmosphere (atmosphere, not tendency!). And this atmosphere in no way detracts from either his artistic power or his psychological perception—on the contrary, it deepens both. For it arose from a very different spiritual background from that of most of the writers of his day.

A moralist, psychologist, student of politics and writer of adventure-stories—quite an unusual combination to find among the highly specialised novelists of the twentieth century! There is, indeed, in Conrad a universalism not of his day—a kind of Renaissance all-roundness and abundance reminiscent of Rabelais and Cervantes, who, in one book, were fabulists, moralists, humorists, and heaven knows what else. Although it is often the universality of genius which raises it above mere talent, I shall not be content to repeat generalities about the mystery of genius. I shall point instead to two definite factors in this spiritual attitude: first, that Conrad may have owed much to the fact that he came of a relatively young race, less sophisticated and more dynamic than the ageing races of Western Europe; and, secondly, that the hard discipline of a sailor's life, and the company of simple people, for

*_To my brethren of the pen_, letter to Mr. W. R. Kane of 19th November 1919. Privately printed.

twenty of his most impressionable years, may have played an important part. This beginning of adult life made it possible for him to retain the insatiable curiosity and the essential uniformity of a primitive nature. Although later he became one of the most sophisticated and many-sided European writers, it was certainly due to this indomitable zest for life, the freshness of his impressions, and, let us add, a sailor's unequivocal moral code, that both adventure and the innermost recesses of the soul never ceased to interest and enthral him, and that, in judging men's actions, he took as his standards the inflexible principles of right and wrong. Conrad was indeed a "whole" man—one not yet split up or developed one-sidedly by the departmentalised civilisation of his day.

This wholeness explains his unusual quality as a writer and a man—his power of attracting and retaining followers, and his right to leadership in the tortuous labyrinth of the modern world. Here, too, is the secret of his distinctiveness—indeed, his uniqueness—which moved one English critic to regret that Conrad never founded a school.

Initiation into Conrad

When I say that Conrad's style, taken as a whole, calls for a certain initiation on the part of the reader, I am not of course thinking of the many wonderful passages which make a direct and instant appeal to everyone. I will explain what I have in mind.

We all know that our impressions of a work of art depend, not only on its objective merits, but on our attitude towards it—in other words, on our mood when the impressions were formed. Our response is also affected by the suitability of the book for us personally—by the extent to which it meets our emotional and intellectual needs. In an aesthetic impression, there is also an element, midway between the objective and the subjective, of which we are less conscious. I am thinking of one's faith in a writer, one's whole attitude to him, and ability to enter into the atmosphere of his work, which largely determines one's opinion of it. We all find that we begin to like and understand certain books only if we come to know them better on re-reading them in a more perceptive frame of mind. It is this kind of attitude that throws the right light on and brings out the true quality of a work which, at a first glance, seemed obscure, pretentious or outdated. Such an attitude may be defined as an initiation. To the uninitiated, things that are full of hidden meanings may seem quite ordinary and pointless.

Conrad's books are, perhaps, the best example one could find of the need for this sort of initiation. Inspired and disdainful writer that he was, he may often, to begin with, seem inflated or morbid, but as we read on and really get into him, we see that he is entitled to his aloofness and scorn.

My own initiation into Conrad lasted several years. I remember feeling at first that his style was forced and that he was straining after a destructive humour that, to me, was not in the least amusing, after would-be profound observations that seemed commonplaces enunciated with great solemnity, after a casualness of expression which I felt was contrived.

There are, of course, times when it cost Conrad a certain effort to get into his stride. He himself admitted that writing was often a nightmare to him; he did not always find it easy to get started; and sometimes, at the beginning, he got stuck. And there is another thing that may mislead us. I think that, especially when he was speaking through one of his narrators, some of his garrulity and triviality was intentional. He seems at times to have discarded some of his own genius in order to make his narrative more lifelike and natural. I admit that it is precisely this tone of everyday life that often sounds slightly unnatural. It does not seem to have been his strong point.

Today these slight defects—from which, one may add, no great writer is free—not only fail to annoy me, but I hardly notice them. My initiation has been achieved, and Conrad's true greatness gives even his less successful passages a value of their own.

Conrad's Reality

What perhaps strikes us most forcibly in Conrad is the exceptional—indeed, unparalleled—vividness of his descriptions. We remember, years after reading one of his books, every detail in the scenes he describes; we might have been there ourselves. Especially when reading him for the first time, we often feel like exclaiming, "What an amazing sense of reality". Later, when we have come to know him better, we begin to feel that the extraordinary vividness of his descriptions comes, not so much from a keen sense of reality or of the significance of life, as from the exact opposite—a deep-seated doubt about the nature of reality.

It seems that Conrad tried to overcome this doubt by the minute accuracy of his descriptions—an accuracy drawn from his inexhaustible memory of life, fidelity to which was his guiding principle. With a precision that was untiring, endlessly watchful and at times wearisome, he set before us every moment of the action, from the most trivial to the most momentous. We are reminded of a film in slow motion. But all this attention to detail seems to be the result of an inner compulsion rather than of any true involvement in reality. We recall Flaubert, that great realist, who, like Conrad, had in fact no genuine sense of reality, but who was fanatically faithful to the truth of life—which, however, he was always delighted to desert (eg. in *Salammbô)* in favour of glorious colours and noble pathos. If we want to find a true sense of reality—sensuous, direct, yet intuitive—we have to turn to Balzac, Maupassant and the Russian novelists. Conrad himself often spoke of "a romantic sense of reality"—in other words, a sense not only of visible reality but of the reality that is brought into being by one's own imagination and sensibility. It was this reality that Conrad introduced, as by sleight of hand, into his books. He always imparted to life more eloquence, lucidity and meaning than we usually find it to possess.

But there is more than this in Conrad's romantic sense of reality—a feeling, deeply hidden, that it may lead, through the delusions and falsity of outward appearances, to the ultimate truth about life; and that reality, if it exists at all, is only to be found in this romantic concept. I said earlier that in the passion for reality that was so characteristic of Conrad I saw an attempt to give permanence to something which in itself is transient and illusory. In saying this, I left much unsaid. In this passion there was also a longing to seize something beyond the illusion of reality: to define new truths, to express meanings hidden below the surface. Conrad, so to speak, cut deep into visible reality in search of its meaning, its essence. Seen in this way, reality inevitably loses some of its "realness", and becomes a symbol or expression of something much more profound.

In Conrad's expression of his own views—which are usually pessimistic enough—it is hard to find any evidence of this hidden aspect of his vision of life. But when we want to know the truth about a writer, it is his writings that we should consult. And, in

Conrad's case, we must not forget the difference between his earlier period and the later one. The earlier period is marked by a relentless search for truth; the later is rather one of resignation, or simply amusement at the dramatic spectacle presented by life, although the two tendencies remained intermingled to the end.

In connection with the above, I should mention my irresistible impression that, true to life as Conrad's books always are, the reality in them is, so to speak, stylised, and that he over-emphasises some of its characteristic features. There is a hint of make-up—especially in the use of charcoal—about it all. Some of his characters seem even to have a slightly statuesque quality—the more so, as he often refers to them by some classical analogy, which he repeats like a refrain. I shall have more to say about these classical allusions in his books.

Fortunately, this type-casting or formalisation of some of Conrad's heroes (Falk—a centaur; Catherine—the Sibyl, in *The Rover;* Jörgensen, a spirit that has strayed into real life in *The Rescue*) is usually confined to visible and external characteristics; the psychology remains vivid and changeable. These figures even have a certain charm of their own, as being a blend of type and character.

I will go further: I think that one can even speak of the theatricality of Conrad, which includes this tendency to type-cast and to see his characters and their conflicts in sharp focus. Indeed, he often presented life as a theatrical production. In *A Personal Record* he put forward the theory that perhaps life had no other meaning than to be a spectacle.

But life looked at this way, ceases to be real. And this is what we feel when we read Conrad. All his terrifyingly convincing realism has in it some suggestion of the unreal, the phantasmagoric, as if it is only by going beyond reality that the author can hope to find firm ground to stand on.

I have spoken of the important part played in Conrad's books by the comparisons he drew with the figures of classical mythology. Here again, we feel his desire to express reality more tellingly—to give it a deeper meaning by linking it with the world of imperishable symbols. His imagination was clearly enthralled by the splendour and power of this legendary world, and he showed consummate artistry in using the accepted meaning of mythological symbols, and, by blending them with the characters in his books, defining these characters more sharply and tellingly. This gift of interconnection, so typical of Conrad, has its charms. It enabled him to become the creator of a contemporary mythology—the begetter of new myths.

To conclude these remarks on Conrad's vision and portrayal of the world, it should be added that the whole nature of his imagination and emotions changed visibly over the years, undergoing a kind of evolution from the phenomenal or even nightmarish to the monumental. His outlook, in the early years, was greatly affected by mood and the compulsive force of his feelings, so that the world, as he saw it, sometimes took on grotesque or ominous forms, which change and vacillate under our eyes, like objects seen in a distorting glass. Their reality is the reality of a nightmare. We need only recall *An Outcast*, "Karain", and *Heart of Darkness*—although we have, at the same time, the temperate and balanced *The Nigger of the 'Narcissus'*. In his later writing (for instance, in *Victory* or *The Rover*), the beings of the world that Conrad created took on definite and unchanging shapes, of a monumental solidity. We might almost say that the world, as he saw it in his early creative years, was like a dream— and sometimes like a nightmare; whereas his later vision of it suggests a brilliantly composed and carefully executed painting. The first was the work of strong feeling; the second, of reflection, and of observation of life as a spectacle. Throughout both periods, however, Conrad was not so much a spectator as a visionary; the power of his imagination dominated both phases and changed reality into its own trans-realistic image. The more, however, 've read of Conrad, the more unreservedly we accept that such is indeed the truth about life. Herein lies the triumph of his art.

Pathos in Conrad

Conrad's power as a master of pathos is widely recognised. It is one of the attractions of his style. Pathos of such true dignity— pathos that is at once sincere and restrained (I am speaking of course of his later writings) is rare: no other element in art so often lends itself to exaggeration. Nothing is more irritating than false pathos, or even pathos that is overdone; even the pathos of that great artist, Victor Hugo, soon gets on one's nerves. We can find it also in abundance in the early Conrad. However, his emotional Polish nature, disciplined by English self-restraint, and further brought under the control of a clear mind, found the *via media* of a disciplined pathos that sounded convincing to his English readers.

In this connection, we must not forget Shakespeare, to whom Conrad undoubtedly owed much of the pathetic cadence of his prose, and, in general, of his striking and very un-Victorian English style. Conrad, while still a child, had imbibed his love of Shakespeare from his father, who had translated a few plays by the great dramatist into Polish. Shakespeare's complete works, in one volume, later accompanied Conrad all over the world, and taught him the language of English literature. We cannot wonder that some of Shakespeare's noble eloquence and titanic vision of life impressed itself on Conrad's style and creative imagination. An attentive reader cannot fail to detect the influence.

Pathos walks a tightrope over a chasm. The fact that Conrad usually kept his footing was due to several factors—the first being the sincerity and depth of the emotion he was expressing: one can always feel the truth behind the words. Secondly, his attitude to creative writing, an attitude independent of all accepted canons and conventions, made it possible for him to follow his own artistic intuition freely and surely; and nothing but the intuition of a great artist could have guided him along the one narrow track that led over these vertiginous heights.

The Rhythm of Conrad's Prose

As soon as one starts reading Conrad, one is struck by the peculiar rhythm of his prose. This rhythm, which he owed, to some extent, to his emotional Polish nature and to Poland's romantic poetry, must, to English readers, have been one of the unconventional and attractive features in this foreigner's use of their own language.

I am speaking, of course, of the distinctive rhythm of prose, which has nothing in common with that of poetry—the rhythm of prose, with its pulsating language, its slow cadences alternating with the restless haste and sudden transitions which so wonderfully convey the emotion throbbing in the words. We may say, indeed, that the rhythm of prose is the expression of its emotional tension. It is an indispensable means of conveying the feelings and moods which inspired it.

The Cradle of Language

In the literature of almost every nation there are some writers, "foreign" by birth, who acquired new languages fairly late in life, and write fairly well in them. But they always write as foreigners, who never completely fit in. Their use of words usually lacks creative power; their vocabulary remains limited and commonplace. Conrad's case is unique, for he was twenty-one when he learnt the language in which he was to make his name as one of its great writers.

Wherein lies the difficulty and wonder of it all? Creative writing necessarily depends on the author's ability to find the exact words for the events and feelings that he wants to describe. The process is almost automatic. There is, as a rule, no need for the author to search for words—they just "come", as though evoked spontaneously by the mood or scene. At most, when the author is turning over possible words in his mind, he suddenly hits on the right one and immediately recognises it as such. This mysterious, indissoluble bond between word and object is formed in early childhood, when we wonderingly begin to discover the world of things and the world of words, and our childish minds first witness that unforgettable encounter between the object and the word which expresses it. As regards the more complex and subtle forms of speech, the process continues far beyond the period of early childhood. But the whole point of the process is its spontaneity—the shock of discovery which, by linking the object with its name, leaves an indelible imprint on the mind.

The case is completely altered when, having, so to speak, imbibed one's own language unconsciously, one acquires another by deliberately learning it. The things of the world and the soul are already known to one by their familiar and irreplaceable names. The new linguistic process is necessarily intellectual, not emotional. The newly acquired words, comprehensible though they are, do not at once form relevant mental pictures or arouse emotions; or, if they finally do so, it is only gradually and indirectly. Such words, and the colourless images connected with them, can never be an ideal material for a writer. He cannot abandon his mother-tongue without becoming, as it were, psychologically tongue-tied; the vital link between himself and the word which is the vehicle of his art has been severed.

These preliminary remarks are meant to show just how

extraordinary a phenomenon Conrad was. They will also help us to see how he came to be a unique exception.

The world, and the sort of life that Conrad led after leaving Poland—a life of ships, the sea, and exotic countries—were something entirely new to him, something outside his experience—a world which had as yet no name. And the language which he heard all round him, and which supplied him with names for all the unfamiliar phenomena and impressions, was equally new to him. He had, indeed, spent three years at sea before he started sailing in English ships, but it was only then that he was really initiated into the ocean and the life of a sailor; up to that time he had been something of an amateur. But thenceforth the new, extraordinary world, and the impressions made on him by his seafaring life, began to link up, for the future master of English prose, with the words used to describe them: reality and expression merged together, organically and indissolubly, as in childhood. Two other factors should also be stressed—the spellbinding strangeness of the world that Conrad was now seeing for the first time, and the extreme—and truly childlike—sensibility of the man who saw it. This sensibility is shown very clearly in the short story, "Youth", which reflects his mood at the time. We must remember, too, his complete severance from the world he had once known—a severance which left the lonely voyager exposed to the strong, almost mesmeric, influence of his new language.

It is significant, too, that Conrad learnt the language of his future literary career in as hard a school as that of a sailor's life, and from simple people. Words learnt in the laborious struggle with a reality that has to be subdued—essential words on which one's life may depend—become as closely linked with reality as the words that one learns in childhood from the sheer joy of learning. Moreover, it seems to me that the fundamental knowledge of, or, more precisely, the intuitive feeling for a new language is best acquired where every language begins—in the daily speech of the people, rather than in the cultured or literary form into which it later crystallises.

This, as I see it, is how the author of *Lord Jim* learnt the language of his art. I am not, of course, forgetting the mysterious factor of genius. Quite a few *émigrés* with a gift for writing must have been in Conrad's position, but they never became Conrads.

The Origin of Conrad's Narrative Technique

Much has been written about the technique of Conrad's books, in which the structure as a whole is gradually built up out of disconnected elements scattered over a period of time. The explanation most often given for his choice of this form is that he was influenced by Henry James and Sterne.

I myself think that there were not less than four factors in Conrad's life which affected the development of this technique so strongly as to make any literary influence of little importance. These factors I will list below.

1. It is almost a commonplace to point out that Conrad's narrative technique closely resembled the way in which people talk over past events—a fact which need not surprise us in a writer who led a very active life before he began to write. He had a dramatic childhood and later sailed all over the world for twenty years, during which he stored up innumerable impressions and experiences. He had plenty to write about, and this adventurous past may have suggested to him the form of the literary yarn as the most natural and appropriate artistic technique for his stories.

This is the way in which many people record their memories. But in Conrad's case it was a genius who remembered. His ability to remember was tremendous. When reading Conrad one has the impression that the whole past lived simultaneously in his memory. He saw everything as from a platform overlooking a vast panorama; he looked at it calmly and from all angles, and described it precisely and without hurry. He was never completely carried away by the scene he was describing, as someone might be who saw it for the first time; and this slight aloofness made him the better able to analyse it, use it creatively, and colour it with his later moods and thoughts. Having complete control over his vision, he reconstructed it, quietly and methodically, out of the riches of his amazing memory and wonderful imagination.

It was not first love; life no longer held for Conrad the charm that it had had in his youth. He now kept his distance from the thing he was describing. His vision of life, a vision halfway between pure creation and memory, had its own charm—the charm of things that are at once familiar and distant—things lived through anew, but which have been assessed by a mature judgement.

2. If we want to trace another factor that may have helped to form Conrad's narrative technique, we should read in quick

succession, first his *Personal Record,* and then Alexander Fredro's memoirs, *Trzy po Trzy.** As we read the great humorist's fascinating, and all too little-known, notes on his youth, we feel like exclaiming, in spite of the chronological evidence, "How extraordinarily well he imitates Conrad!"

There is indeed an astonishing resemblance between the form of Conrad's memoirs and that of Fredro. We find in both the same discursive inconsequence, at the mercy of the writer's imagination; the same casual way of tying up loose threads by means of a chance image, or even word; the same disregard for chronology; the same slow, sauntering way of telling a story; the same habit of circling round some event or theme. Even the opening passages of the two memoirs—in Conrad's, an incident in the steamer, the Adowa; in Fredro's, a moment, chosen at random, in the campaign of 1813— are strangely alike in the apparently fortuitous singling-out of the events that they record. In fact, the books of both men show the characteristics of the old Polish *gavenda,* marvellously transmuted into works of art.†

As I have pointed out, Conrad's own form of *gavenda* is often attributed to the influence of Sterne's *Tristram Shandy.* But Sterne's influence cannot account for the fact that Conrad's and Fredro's reminiscences are, in mood and style, far more like each other than either is like Sterne. And there is no evidence of Conrad's reading Fredro's memoirs before he wrote his own. It is hard, then, to doubt the impression made on both Fredro and Conrad by the tradition of the old Polish *gavenda,* and by the

---

*Alexander Fredro (1793-1876) was a famous writer of comedies who won the reputation of being the Polish Molière. He fought in the Napoleonic wars. His best-known comedies were written around the year 1830, but his book of memories, *Trzy po Trzy* (Topsy-turvy Talk), was not written until 1848, when he had settled down on his country estate. It was published posthumously in 1877 and reprinted in 1917.

†The *gavenda,* although related to similar types of literary "yarn" in other countries, had, by the eighteenth century, developed into a specifically Polish genre of narrative, which later, particulary during the Romantic period, was much used by Polish writers. The best English definition of *gavenda* that I can think of is "rambling narrative" or "literary yarn". It might be helpful to quote the definition given by Andrzej Busza in his book, *Conrad's Polish Literary Background, and Some Illustrations of the Influence of Polish Literature on his Work,* (Rome 1966).
    'The "gawenda" is a loose, informal narrative, told by a speaker in the manner of someone reminiscing. It is often involved and full of digressions. At first, seemingly unimportant details and fragmentary episodes come to the fore; then gradually a coherent picture emerges. This form of narration, originating from an oral tradition, first appeared in Polish literature during the Romantic period. It was used both in poetry and prose...'
    Having thus explained the meaning of *gavenda,* I shall use the Polish word when discussing Conrad's literary method.

28

works of such masters of the *gavenda* as Rzewuski, Kaczkowski and Pol (all contemporary with Fredro, and very popular during Conrad's youth in Poland).

Professor Wyka, of the Jagellon University in Cracow, came independently to the same conclusion—namely, that Conrad was influenced by the Polish *gavenda* style of narrative. I quote from Professor Wyka's study, *Czas Powieściowy* (Time in the Novel), Warsaw, 1969: "The teller of *gavenda* in bygone Poland left descendents. His great-great-great-grandson is Conrad's mouthpiece, Marlow. To test the truth of this statement, let us consider the literature out of which Conrad's books grew. He was steeped, in his youth, in the French novelists; he always retained a humble respect for Flaubert, and greatly admired Turgenev and Dickens. But from his very first book—more, indeed, in his early books than in his later ones—he consistently presented his narrative in the form characteristic of the *gavenda* of Polish Romantic fiction. His own answer to the impersonal, restrained, objective narrative of the great novelists of the West, whom he himself admired so much, is Marlow. There is a clear line of descent running from Rzewuski, Kaczkowski and the other writers of *gavenda* in the first half of the nineteenth century, right down to Marlow. To put it in a nutshell: between Conrad's narrative form, and the narrative traditions of Polish prose, there is less difference than that which exists between his narrative form and the narrative traditions of fiction in Western Europe."

3. It is interesting, too, to note the resemblances between, on the one hand, the old Polish *gavenda* and Conrad's story-telling, and, on the other hand, the stories in the *Arabian Nights,* with their leisureliness and interwoven themes. We see a similar technique in, for instance, the classical *Golden Ass* of Apuleius— that vivid tapestry of endlessly intersecting threads. Then we come to the stories of the Renaissance, those of Boccaccio or the Queen of Navarre; for even the *Decameron,* that series of tales held together by a single situation, comes into the same category.

There is an obvious resemblance of form, and even of theme, in these old collections of stories; and although it is, to some extent, due to mutual influence—the influence of the Eastern tales being particularly strong—the real explanation surely lies in the type of civilisation in which, centuries ago, the art of story-telling developed. It is easy to guess what gave this literary form the leisurely pace, the diversified nature and the intricacy which also characterise the *gavenda*. People had plenty of time, and there was no need for them to hurry over their story-telling; they could, if they felt like it, digress, confident that, however long the digression might be, they would always be able to bring their tale to an end. Unlike us today, they had not been caught up in the wheels of time. Time, to them, was something relatively unimportant: they took it lightly, had a tendency to play with it, and often forgot it altogether.

Nor was this casual attitude to time the only feature that the earlier writers had in common; they also stood at a certain distance, both emotionally and factually, from their theme. In those days, the great world and the main current of life were so far removed from the restricted ground of most men's experience that there seemed little connection between them. Today, everything is affected by everything else, and it becomes increasingly difficult to find a secluded corner from which to watch the distant panorama of life. The story-teller of the past looked on, untroubled, at events taking place far from him, or at those which, long ago, he had himself experienced, and which were now past and done with. This is why the old *gavenda* gave a sense of peace, of almost playing with life. It came into being at the fireside, and there, during the long winter evenings, it flourished. From these homely beginnings it was carried far and wide by roving story-tellers and minstrels, who always found a crowd of idlers ready to listen to them.

The art of the *gavenda,* which died out with the circumstances which gave rise to it, survived longer and developed more local characteristics in Poland than anywhere else. This may have been because it was particularly suited to the volatility of the Polish imagination. Poland, moreover, remained a backwater far longer than most of Europe—and, as we have seen, this setting is essential to the *gavenda*.

4. I have pointed out the connecting link between the *gavenda*-like form of Conrad's books and the spirit of the old Polish *gavenda*. What I have just written suggests yet another source of this form in Conrad's books—the influence of his life at sea. The analogy is obvious. The point of vantage from which he observed life did not greatly differ from that of the ancient writers. Sailing-ships made an ideal setting for the development of his gifts as a story-teller. In the peaceful periods of an ocean voyage there is plenty of free time, and the world is very far away. Conrad once told Retinger that he began to write as a way of killing time when

he was off duty. Men in a fo'c'sle chat as they do by the fireside, and there is nothing to hurry or interrupt either the narrator or his listeners. It was at sea that Conrad learnt his disregard of time, and freed himself for ever from the bondage in which it holds landsmen. Time became something outside himself—something in which he was not involved. It was at sea, too, that he acquired the habit of looking at life from a distance, as something that had happened in the past, or perhaps was happening then, but far away, on land, and which could therefore be looked at dispassionately and objectively.

The second half of Conrad's life—the half devoted to writing—did nothing to alter his attitude to the world. He lived in the country and seldom left it, but even if he had not been cut off from the main current of events by his surroundings, he would have been so in spirit, for he lived in his memories, which he transformed into art. Thus the tendency to spin yarns that he had acquired at sea was strengthened by his later attitude to life as to a past outside time, which lay irrevocably behind him.

Conrad's Isolation

Any man who lives cut off from other people ends by talking to himself; mentally, indeed, he does so almost from the start. It is not an act of the will, but a subconscious means of defence against loneliness, and the fear which, sooner of later, lurks in all loneliness. A lonely man must either bemuse himself with work, or talk to himself, if he is to hold off the void surrounding him. He has to interpose something that will keep it from him—to fill it with at least the sound of his own voice and the flow of his own thoughts. If he once stops thinking and working, solitude, from being external, will pierce right through him; and that, no one can endure.

We know that Conrad was by nature solitary, if only in the sense that he never lost the feeling of being a stranger in the world that he had chosen for himself. In any case, this sense of estrangement and loneliness was very real to him in the twenty years of his wanderings.

Tragedies caused by loneliness occur repeatedly in his books. "Who knows what true loneliness is—not the conventional word, but the naked terror?"* he asks in *Under Western Eyes*. In *An*

Under Western Eyes, p. 39.

Outcast of the Islands, Willems nearly goes mad when Lingard abandons him in the jungle. Decoud, in *Nostromo,* shoots himself on his lonely island. Behind these unforgettable creative visions there must lie an enormous number of Conrad's own experiences, from his lonely night watches at sea to the most subtle manifestations of the "naked terror" of solitude. No doubt he, like everyone else, sought protection from this threat by carrying on interminable conversations with himself, and filling his solitude with a constant flow of thoughts, fancies and memories.

It was not only Conrad's inborn creative genius, not only the enthralling memories that clamoured for expression, that turned him into a teller of tales. They poured from him, first for his own entertainment, and later on for other audiences, near and far (we are again reminded of the origin of the *gavenda*). These were not the only reasons for his writing; equally insistent, no doubt, was the need to battle against loneliness, to hold it from him by interposing the characters and events conjured up by his imagination.

We may recall how often—from the famous apparition of Almayer onwards—Conrad speaks of being visited by his own fictional characters, summoned, one might suppose, to bear him company in his loneliness.

The School of the Primitive

The anthropologist, Bronisław Malinowski, a Pole whose contribution to English learning may be compared, *toutes proportions gardées,* with that of Conrad to English literature, invented a new method of conducting research into sociological phenomena. This, the ·functional method, consists of studying these phenomena where they first developed—i.e. among primitive peoples—and applying the principles thus deduced to societies at more advanced stages of development.

It is interesting to note that Conrad's genius took much the same line. We recall his accurate and vivid descriptions of the small-scale politics in the semi-civilised petty kingdoms of the Malay States (Sambir in *Almayer's Folly,* Patusan in *Lord Jim,* the state of Wajo in *The Rescue*). Only then are we able to explain, to a certain extent, the phenomenon of *Nostromo*—that most profound and many-sided of all the novels written in our day on social and political problems. We may surmise that Conrad, by observing the customs of primitive peoples, learnt, from their ingenuous, uncomplicated example, the structure of social life in general. This is not all, however. Life on board, and contacts with uncivilised countries, where he encountered mankind in its early, simplified form, may have given Conrad, both as a psychologist and an artist, something even more fundamental and important than an early insight into the patterns of social life.

When a sensitive person, as yet immature, is confronted with the complexity and many-sidedness of a highly advanced civilisation, he is often in danger of mental and moral disorientation and disintegration. But among the crew of the *Narcissus*, or in villages on the outskirts of a jungle, a perceptive mind soon acquires a basic knowledge of the main elements of human behaviour, and the principal laws by which mankind is governed. When such a mind later faces more complex problems and forms of life, it has its methods of observation and its schemes all ready, and is at once able to understand and classify matters that are far more intricate.

Conrad's time at sea served him as a kind of beginner's course, in which his powers of observation developed into the ability to understand the complexities of men as members of society.

A link between the old and new

To return to my starting point—Conrad as a figure of the Renaissance. He re-introduced in his works the classical, ever-valid methods of art, much as the masters of the Renaissance had opened the eyes of their contemporaries to the values of antiquity. Things which, in his day, might have seemed hopelessy out-dated and fit only for books for boys or the uneducated—such things as melodrama, the charm of *gavenda*, hero-worship, a clearly defined moral code—all this took on new life under the magic of his pen. Art was, in its origins, a simplified, clear-cut and dramatic presentation of life. It takes a master like Conrad to prevent these age-old methods from seeming outmoded; above all, it takes a great soul to give them the ring of truth.

Yet this writer, who made such generous use of the old traditions of art, was simultaneously one of the most acute observers and critics of contemporary life—a forerunner of Sartre and Camus in his descriptions of the bewilderment and anguish of man today and an inventor of the new, sophisticated forms of the modern novel. He is thus a true link between the past and the present. Man's thought, as well as his art, will often look back at that lonely writer, who never founded a school.

CONRAD AND SARTRE: TWO ETHICS OPPOSED

There is no better way of obtaining a deeper insight into a man's mind and personality than by comparing him with another personality of similar stature — particularly if there are not only resemblances but marked differences between the two men. The comparison brings out the characteristic features of both. This is especially true in the case of Sartre, the post-war prophet of existentialism, and Conrad. Let us start with a brief comparison between their outlooks on life.

Sartre: Man finds himself in this world — how or why, nobody knows: quite simply, here he is. That is the only ascertainable fact. He has no authority behind him, no example before him; there is neither God nor law. No one, therefore, can help him, and he is accountable to no one. The one sure thing on which he can rely is the fact of his existence.

In this alien, dreary, hostile world, where everything threatens his existence, and where certain death lies at the end, man is ceaselessly dogged by anxiety, disgust and fear — fear, not only of the dangers that may be in store for him, but of the mere fact of his existence.

In this hopeless situation, what is there left for him? One thing only — to make the very most of the freedom which he did not choose, "to which he was condemned", but which is none the less his — absolute freedom from every law and moral obligation. It is left to him to create, somehow, by his own will, a complete self out of a chance being, stranded in the void. Man must, then, make unending choices among the possibilities that life sets before him, for these choices will determine what he becomes. The difficulty lies in the fact that, while it is his duty to choose and make decisions, he has no real grounds on which to base his choice. "There are no signs in heaven" — to quote Sartre's own words. There are no general laws to show how one ought to live. There is no good, nor evil. Any choice, as long as it is made in the name of freedom, is as good as any other. What, then, is the final purpose of this incessant choosing? Simply that one may "surpass" oneself, become more than one is.

Conrad: The world has no ethical purpose. Perhaps it is a mere spectacle, without either meaning or order. The actors in this dreary spectacle live in almost unceasing anguish — the anguish of loneliness, guilt, and so on. For every gleam of happiness, one has to pay with suffering, if not with death. Is there any way out of this nightmare of life? Only by devoting oneself tirelessly to the tasks one has undertaken, however inconspicuous they may be — by doing one's duty to the last, and thus keeping one's balance over the abyss of life, without falling into its murky depths.

To act thus is to find, against all the odds, a worthy aim in one's life — to find it by one's passion for, and loyalty to, things that are near and concrete, as though they were sublime and of immense importance. It is only thus that man, weak and imperfect as he is by nature, can retain what is most precious in life—dignity and self-respect.

As we see, the two writers start from the same point and share the same gloomy view of existence as a meaningless void in which man's lonely destiny works itself out. Sartre, and the other existentialist writers, vie with each other in describing the squalor and repulsiveness of life, and man's helplessness, terror and despair in the face of it. Conrad's artistic methods differ from those of Sartre, but the essence is the same. Sartre himself does not give us such unforgettable pictures of the drama of existence, or convey so piercingly the sense of loneliness, fear and guilt. Even the revulsion typical of Sartre finds a parallel in Conrad (the "horror" of Kurtz; the "disgust" of Heyst).

Again, the reaction of Conrad and Sartre is similar: not to give in, but to put up a fight, to struggle out of the trap. Both were fighters by nature, although in different ways and for different reasons.

Finally, their philosophy of life can be traced back to the same origin, the same atmosphere. It is common knowledge that one's outlook on life is, to a great extent, the reflection of one's emotional experience. The concept of existence shared by Conrad and Sartre was in all probability forced on them by the defeat of their respective countries and the brutal oppresion of the invaders — an oppression transformed in the minds of both writers into a sense of metaphysical oppression by existence itself. This was aggravated by the hopelessness, uncertainty and disorder that followed defeat. Both men must have asked themselves the despairing question: What is to be done now, when all seems lost? We already know the answers that they gave.

It was the German occupation of France that established Sartre as a writer. Conrad was a child of the atmosphere which prevailed in Poland after the Rising of 1863. His outlook on life was formed by the tragedy of his nation, and by his own drama — that of a homeless exile, haunted by a feeling of loneliness and remorse at having abandoned his country.

The philosophy and art of both writers were thus a philosophy and an art of defeat, of failure in life, and of the resultant despair which destroys all conscious faith in the meaning of life and the existence of someone — a good and just someone — who is above life. Man is alone in a hostile world. Everything, and everyone, has abandoned him. He must simply make the best of what he has.

Here the resemblances between the two writers end. Sartre, oppressed by life, tells us to cast off the remaining fetters which restrain our freedom: Conrad, to tighten them. Sartre's conviction seems to be that we can only find liberation by rejecting all the traditions and laws brought into being by centuries of civilisation. Conrad makes a deliberate choice from the inheritance of the past, and abides, with unflinching fidelity, by what he has chosen.

Conrad is, without doubt, more mature and far-seeing than Sartre. Perhaps, as the son of a nation which, over the centuries, has been so often in bondage, but never succumbed, he inherited more stamina and experience to enable him to endure and rise up from the very depths of oppression and despair. We should also remember that he spent twenty years of his early life on ships in the hard school of the sea — a school of discipline and danger. He knew that the only armour which strengthens and heartens a man is the armour that he himself has put on voluntarily. He tried therefore to introduce his own sense of law and order into a lawless and undisciplined world. Men, in Conrad's books, submit willingly to every form of discipline — that of honour, duty and integrity — to prevent themselves from going to pieces: they submit precisely because they are indeed on their own, answerable only to themselves, with no one to compel them, and no one, and nothing, to protect them. They are inspired by the same defensive instinct which leads people living in dangerous conditions, far from the civilised world, to impose on themselves, for their own survival, a strict moral discipline. Kierkegaard himself, the precursor of existentialism, wrote in his diary: "What is of utmost importance is to maintain in the life of the individual as many as possible of the universal qualities of man". This is just what Conrad does. Out of the prevailing chaos, out of psychological defeat, he seeks to perpetuate the supreme achievements of mankind — moral discipline and humanitarianism.

Where Sartre fails, Conrad succeeds. It was all very well for Sartre to preach freedom, but his books never gave the reader any sense of it; on the contrary, they dragged him further and further into an obsession with the nightmare-like quality of existence, and ended by destroying all his will and hope. Conrad's sombre picture of life makes one long for liberation, and stimulates the will to fight for it. Thus, in the darkness of life's night, Conrad saves our faith in man.

It is the standard we apply to life that matters, not what is measured by this standard. In even the most pessimistic of Conrad's books, we find this inviolable standard. The crisis of values, which shook the very foundations of the writer's belief in a moral sense of existence, was unable to shake the solid foundations of his own soul. Hence the strange paradox so typical of Conrad — his sense of the pointlessness of life side by side with his insistence on the need for a moral code by which to regulate it: hence, too, Conrad's own balanced judgement, clearly defined standards, and deep human compassion. The order which dominates his work from within, and the light falling on it from above, prevent the reader from losing his way in the darkness, and make him feel that he is following a trustworthy guide, and that, sooner or later, the night will end.

Conrad's hour has come. A facile idealism cannot survive, faced with the appalling reality of life today. Only an idealism that is stern, inflexible and free from illusions can challenge the prevailing gloom — just as the poor, inured to hunger, hold out longest in a famine.

To sum up. Sartre's portrayal of life crushes and paralyses the reader; Conrad's, like frosty air, braces him and whips up his energy. It is Conrad, not Sartre, who can show us the narrow track leading out of the post-war world of defeat and anarchy. Stripped of illusions as he was, but still fighting on in defence of man's noblest qualities, Conrad becomes a guide through the shadows.

THE DUALITY IN CONRAD

In the second half of 1901, during one of Conrad's most creative periods, he wrote, in between *Lord Jim* and *Nostromo*, two short stories based on the fundamental conflict in his life.

The intensely personal nature of the first of these stories, "Amy Foster", has long been recognised. The fact that Conrad tried, twice, to turn the second story, "To-morrow", into a play — and did so twenty years later — seems sufficient proof that it, too, was of special significance to him.

The stories are noteworthy for the simplicity of both subject and treatment. One of the marks of Conrad's genius was precisely his ability to convey the deepest and most intimate truths about himself and life in general by means of situations that are at times so simple and natural that they appear to be mere fragments of reality, presented without any artifice. *Heart of Darkness*, that devastating attack on European civilization, is simply a record of a trading journey to the Congo. "The Secret Sharer", one of the most complex — and most often discussed — pieces of literary symbolism, is just the story of an adventure at sea. We find the same simplicity in the two stories I mentioned at the beginning of this chapter. Conrad knew how to express in them, completely and with great clarity, the two unreconciled and irreconcilable sides of his character — his response to the unceasing call of wide distances, and the incurable loneliness of the wanderer.

His problem was the ambivalence, the eternal contradiction inherent in the drama of his life. It had driven him out of Poland and brought on him reproaches from without and torment within himself. It never left him free to enjoy those wanderings over the face of the earth that he had chosen as his life. And, finally, it was, indirectly as well as directly, the seminal force of his creativity.

It was not, as we know, the only conflict that tore him apart. He was remarkable for the ambivalence of almost all his feelings. Perhaps it was only the fact that he could, as a writer, transfer his inner tensions to his work, that enabled him to preserve his psychological equilibrium.

"Amy Foster" preceded "To-morrow" by a few months. Conrad began it in June 1910, just after he had finished "Falk". "Amy Foster" is the story of a Polish immigrant cast up on the English coast, like a wild bird from the Tatra mountains. The stranger never felt at home in the country of his chance adoption, and died asking for the glass of water that no one gave him because no one could understand what he wanted. The whole story is a dramatised confession. We know from Conrad's wife that he himself, when in high fever, raved in Polish, and that she was as much alarmed as Amy Foster.

"To-morrow" is the story of a sailor's visit to his family — a visit that he could not endure for more than a few hours. This contrapuntal apologia for freedom from home ties, written soon after "Amy Foster", expressed the other side of Conrad's nature — the side that had led him, as a small boy, to put his finger on a map of Africa and say "I shall go *there*", and which later drove him out of his own country and sent him wandering over the face of the earth. The house in "To-morrow" is stuffy, dreary and crazy; the far distance is gay and enticing.

Conrad swung, then, unceasingly from a positive to a negative attitude to the life he had chosen, and solved the problem, in a creative dream, now in one way and now in another.

Comment on the two stories is unnecessary. They speak for themselves; any discussion of them would dilute and weaken their eloquence. In their simple, expressive symbolism they are unique, comprising in their brevity the dialogue that Conrad carried on within himself, and which did not cease even towards the end of his life. As an elderly man he had a sudden longing to go off on a whaling expedition to the Arctic Ocean while at the same time dreaming — as his wife tells us — of leaving England and "settling down for good in his beloved country".

It is certain that in "To-morrow" and "Amy Foster" Conrad deliberately contrasted these two attidudes to life even if it was a sudden impulse that brought the stories into being. As a work of art, "To-morrow" cannot be compared with the perfection of "Amy Foster". This, however, was something that lay outside the author's intention, and it does not alter the nature of that intention. Both stories, as I have said, were written in the same short space of time, and appeared in the same collection (*Typhoon and Other Stories*). Conrad even chose the same setting for both stories — the country around Colebrook, a small seaside town in Kent. These resemblances show not only a similar emotional basis, but also a deliberate contrasting of the two themes.

The same elements — the joy of seeing the world, and the eternal loneliness of the wanderer — are, of course, scattered throughout Conrad's writings, from "Youth" to *Victory*. But in these two stories in the *Typhoon* collection, Conrad gave what is perhaps the purest and most complete expression to the dual nature within him; one almost feels that in these stories he wrote a motto (he liked mottoes!) for the book of his life.

This is why, in my "psychological" biography of the author of *Lord Jim*, I could not pass over "Amy Foster" and "To-morrow" without at least a few words of comment.

Conrad before leaving Poland (1873).

41

CONRAD AT HOME

Jessie Conrad's memoirs* of her husband have not a high reputation. They are usually regarded as trivial, superficial, and at times inaccurate. Even her sons did not think much of her book. It is easy enough to see why. The chorus of condemnation is due to the fact that Jessie concentrated on Conrad's weaknesses, without giving us much idea of his greatness.

Moreover the book is full of self-praise. Whenever Conrad got into difficulties, Jessie always took the credit for getting him out of them, and, according to her, was unfailingly able to do so. This concentration on herself in a book supposed to be about her husband shakes the reader's confidence in her objectivity.

One thing alone, however, should concern the student of Conrad: are the "facts" reported by Jessie essentially true, or are they not?

It is, of course, nothing new to find a discrepancy between the generally accepted view of a man, and the figure he cuts at home. There, with his family, and especially with his wife, he throws off all pretence, as he never does before the outer world.

We all know the expression, "a worm's eye view" — a view from below, from a worm's level. The phrase describes fairly accurately Jessie's account of Conrad. She saw him from her own level — not very perceptively, and without any great depth of understanding; but she noted down, as truthfully as she could, what she saw, as she saw it. I have no doubt that she observed with affection — an affection that was perhaps more maternal than purely feminine — and with the respect due to a great writer; she felt herself under an obligation to give the world a faithful picture of the man who had

---

* I am here referring especially to her second book of memoirs *Joseph Conrad and His Circle*. Her first book, *Joseph Conrad as I Knew Him*, did not tell us much.

shared her life. The confimation of my belief is Conrad's own attitude to her; it was both affectionate and grateful.

The picture she drew, does undoubtedly contain an element of exaggeration. But it is surely impossible to doubt the essential truth of what she wrote. The Conrad who appears in her memoirs is natural and convincing. Jessie could not have invented him; to do so, she would have needed a far deeper understanding than she had of his complex nature, so different from her own and from that of her countrymen. It is this that gives the sense of reality to her descriptions; we feel we are on firm ground. It is for us to supply the understanding and to draw our own conclusions.

I myself value Jessie's memoirs and have learnt a good deal from them. The casual observations of his friends, or even of his sons, who regarded their father with youthful awe do not tell us much about Conrad at home — Conrad *en pantoufles*. It is mainly from Jessie that we learn of this side of him.

Among other things, we see from her memoirs how Polish Conrad remained in his reactions, tastes and behaviour — how very little the years he spent with his English family altered him. On this point Jessie gives us a good deal of interesting material. It is she who tells us that he never lost even the weaknesses of his Polish temperament; the manners and customs of his adopted country did nothing to tone them down. If anything, in fact, they grew more pronounced as time went on. He kept, to the end, his impulsive — at times ungovernable — temperament; his delicate sense of honour, and a somewhat touchy concern for his dignity; his chivalrous attitude to women, and extreme courtesy to all visitors; and last but not least, his lavish hospitality — a hospitality exercised, to Jessie's dismay, with a total disregard to the state of his finances.

Jessie herself no doubt became more or less inured to her husband's strange ways, and increasingly tolerant of his fluctuating moods, particularly as his health began to deteriorate. But even after his death Jessie showed no greater understanding of him.

It would be asking too much of Jessie to expect her, with her background and conventional mind, to show such understanding. She did what she could. She tried, by all the means in her power, to make the life of her difficult husband run smoothly, and to leave a faithful record of what she could not understand.

Conrad was too good a psychologist not to see Jessie's limitations. Probably he had already seen them, when marrying her, and got what he expected. After all she was not a bad wife to him.

Two final comments. What I have said about Conrad's temperament and behaviour should be taken with certain reservations. He was not typical of a Pole from any other part of the country. His type of Polishness was clearly defined. It was that of the gentry who for centuries had been settled in the war-torn borderland ("kresy") of South-Eastern Poland, known for the proud, independent and fiercely patriotic spirit of its people. Conrad was the product of his place and time.

Again, we must remember that the inconsistencies and extremes of his behaviour owed something, not only to the emotional Polish temperament, but to the emotional and egocentric nature of the artist. The two very similar emotional trends reinforced each other. Hence the intensity of their outward manifestations.

Conrad with his family in 1914.

Conrad at his desk in 1914.

PART II
CONRAD, THE POLE

CONRAD'S LIFE THROUGH POLISH EYES

Before one starts a book, it is always illuminating to know something of its author. In the case of the author of *Lord Jim* such knowledge is essential.

Józef Konrad Korzeniowski, had the most "Polish" childhood imaginable. Born of a nation which for nearly a century had been under Russian rule, he was five years old at the time of the 1863 Rising, of which his father, Apollo Korzeniowski, was one of the moving spirits. Apollo was banished to a remote part of Russia, where his wife, who had voluntarily accompanied him, died. Two of Conrad's uncles were killed during the Rising. To complete the picture, his paternal grandfather, an officer in the Polish Legions under Napoleon, had taken part in the Rising of 1831.

The five-year-old Conrad, who went with his parents to Russia, knew what exile meant, and undoubtedly remembered it. He was ten when his father, whose sentence in the meantime had been remitted, returned with shattered health to Poland. Conrad spent the next two years at the bedside of this dearly-loved father, who died in Cracow in 1869.

All who knew Conrad at the time described him as an unusually precocious and sensitive child — the sort of child whom such memories were bound to haunt for life. And the man destined to this heritage was later to write in a foreign language, under an assumed name; to marry a foreigner, and to become the father of children who regarded themselves as English. The situation had all the makings of drama.

Conrad's emotional life was inevitably torn apart. The only period that was not, was that of his sea-going youth — those years of glorious adventure when there was as yet no conflict between the loyalties he owed to his own, and to his adopted, country. This may explain why youth, the one really carefree period, always seemed to him so beautiful, and why he wrote of it so poignantly.

After his father's death, Conrad, under the guardianship of his uncle Bobrowski, lived in Cracow until he was sixteen. Cracow, after the Rising, which had been ruthlessly suppressed, was sunk in the apathy of its national mourning and seemed to hold out little hope for the future. It could not have had much attraction for a gifted boy, eager to discover life for himself. Conrad must have felt stifled by the prevailing atmosphere of hopelessness, made all the more oppressive by his personal tragedy.

We do not precisely know when he decided to break away and make for the open seas, but the decision, once made, was irrevocable, and no opposition from his family could shake him. He was drawn to the sea by his restless poetic imagination, his longing for adventure — the sort of adventure he had read so much about — and perhaps even by a dream of avenging, under the English flag, his father's death and his country's bondage.*

Conrad's longing was strengthened by his sense of hopelessness during the period following the 1863 Rising, by his rebellion against his own powerlessness, and by his desire for freedom and the happiness outlawed by a country in mourning. Jean-Aubry, Conrad's biographer, also writes of a disappointment in love.

It was, then, imagination, restless and unfulfilled, that drove him out to the freedom of the seas — drove him out for ever. He sailed those seas for twenty years — first in the French merchant navy, and later, to the end of his sea-faring life, in the British. But even in Marseilles, where he first saw the sea, he lost his heart to English ships, as he was later to lose it to the English language.

The years 1874-1890 that Conrad spent at sea were the happiest and the only carefree period of his life. It was a period of the alluring adventures and unforgettable emotions that only youth can know. He writes of it very beautifully in "Youth".

According to all accounts, he was an exemplary sailor, and it was while he was at sea that his almost fanatical devotion to the demands of duty and faithful service first became part of him. We see from his writings that during his later years at sea this sense of duty grew steadily stronger, while the illusions and emotions of youth slowly faded away. His health at last broke down after a severe attack of malaria during a voyage up the River Congo.

---

* As suggested by a Polish critic, K. Zawodziński. It should be noted that the England of that day, with her memories of the Crimean War, was consistently hostile to Russia.

Three years later, in 1894, when he was living, out of work, in London, he finished his first novel in English — *Almayer's Folly* — which he had begun at sea. The book shows very clearly the poetic heritage bequeathed to him by his father, and intensified by the exotic countries, alien races and strange adventures that had come his way. He sent it to a firm of publishers, where it had the good fortune to fall into the hands of Edward Garnett, an exceptionally discerning reader, who at once saw its quality, and who later became Conrad's lifelong friend. The book was well received, at least by connoisseurs, and Conrad, who had spent his entire adult life at sea, suddenly became a member of the literary world. The son of Korzeniowski, the ardent Polish patriot, had embarked on the career of an English writer. He had done so almost by chance — partly through the ill-health that had made him take to life ashore, and partly as a result of Garnett's encouragement. In his later writings, Conrad often stresses the element of chance, of unpremeditated impulse rather than conscious decision, in his choice of a literary career. It seems, however, probable that one of the reasons for this emphasis on chance and impulse was his feeling that they had absolved him from the responsibility of making a deliberate choice.

We know very little about Conrad's attitude to Poland's tragic fate during the first — the sea-going — period of his life abroad. There are no letters, documents or passages in his books that throw much light on the question. It is hard to tell whether there was already a conflict between his sense of duty towards Poland and his love of a seafaring life. If any such conflict existed it could not have been very severe. At that time there were no Polish ships for him to sail on; there was no definite obligation to recall him to Poland; and hardly anyone knew or remembered the sailor on the high seas.

The conflict only began when his first book was published in English. It was his choice of a foreign language, not of his maritime profession, that might have been regarded as a renunciation of his country.

And the very next novel he wrote was on the subject of betrayal — the betrayal of his own race by the outcast Willems. The theme of betrayal was to reappear in many of his books. And there is another striking thing. In spite of the success of his first novel, he did not want to write a second; indeed, he insisted that he was returning to the merchant navy. One can see his point: one book could be a sailor's whim; the second would mean his decision to become an English writer. It was his friend Garnett who finally persuaded him to write *An Outcast of the Islands*. His hesitation and reluctance to go on writing in English may have been prompted by a premonition that, if he did so, he would be accused of disloyalty to his country.

The premonition was all too well-founded, and the blow was not long in coming. It took the form of an open letter, in which a well-known Polish novelist, Eliza Orzeszkowa, accused him of betraying his country's cause for financial gain, by putting his talent to the service of another country, when his own, in desperate straits, needed the help of all her people — and especially those with talent.* Conrad remembered the letter to the end of his life. With his usual pride, he never spoke of it, nor did he reply by an open letter of his own. Instead, he wrote *Lord Jim.***

He was to write many books that were more finished as works of art, but into none of them did he put more of himself. In his inward conflict over the charge of betrayal — a conflict which involved his honour, his way of life, and the understanding by others of his tragic situation — he cast off all disguise and spoke out unequivocally.

Lord Jim played a decisive part in the moral drama of Conrad's life. Once he had written it, he was no longer defenceless. He had thought over and elaborated his confession, and presented it to the world; and his confession was his defence. But as far as he himself was concerned, the matter did not end there. The values he had once taken for granted — unswerving loyalty, duty done to the bitter end — had now become the most important things in life to him. He made a cult of moral inflexibility. However sure of defeat a man may be, he must, if he is to keep his self-respect and save his honour, be true to his principles and remain at his post.

Conrad never renounced his nationality. In fact, as time went on and his fame grew, he stressed it increasingly. But he was also a good English citizen and patriot. He came to feel a deep loyalty to two countries — to Poland, who had given him birth, and to England, who had given him a home. It was not an easy position for him, but he found a way of accepting it, and even of making it express an

* The letter appeared in 1899, in a periodical called *Kraj*.
** He was already working on the draft of a short story about the incident on the *Patna*, but it was only after the appearance of Orzeszkowa's letter that this first draft of an ordinary sea story grew into a remarkable novel.

inner truth that aroused faith and respect. Like Lord Jim, he became "happy—nearly" in his adopted country. But towards the end of his life, one of the wishes of which he spoke to his wife was to return to Poland.

CONRAD'S POLISH COMPLEX:
A GENERAL VIEW

Wer den Dichter will verstehen
Muss im Dichters Lande gehen (Goethe)

I begin this chapter by reasserting my conviction that it is impossible to dissociate Conrad's writing from his life, and from the history of his country.

In *Under Western Eyes* Conrad wrote of his hero Razumov: "It is unthinkable that any young Englishman should find himself in Razumov's situation. This being so it would be a vain enterprise to imagine what he would think. The only safe surmise to make is that he would not think as Mr. Razumov thought at this crisis of his fate. He would not have an hereditary and personal knowledge of the means by which a historical autocracy represses ideas, guards its power, and defends its existence".*

The above applies, in reverse, to Conrad's own situation, for he was himself a member of a cruelly oppressed nation.

At the end of the eighteenth century, the history of Poland, formerly one of the great countries of Europe, completely changed its course. In the next hundred and fifty years Poland, having lost her freedom, underwent a profound political transformation that cut her off entirely from the rest of Europe. As a result of this we cannot, when we try to fathom the psychology of one of her great sons, apply the standards that are accepted elsewhere.

If, then, we want to understand Conrad at any depth, we must not only have a good knowledge of the history of his country but be well versed in its tradition. This is particularly true when we come to consider the matter of his leaving Poland.

---

* Under Western Eyes, p. 25.

If a member of a free nation chooses to live in another country, it is his own affair; whether he is a private individual or a famous writer makes no difference. It is another matter when someone leaves a beleaguered city, in which his presence may be of the utmost importance.

In Conrad's day, Poland was a beleaguered city; and his parents had died defending it. This was his moral problem of which he could not be unaware. Had he been, his compatriots would have pointed it out to him. And one of them — Eliza Orzeszkowa — did so in a particularly painful manner.

There were, of course, thousands of Polish émigrés all over the world, and few of them felt any remorse over their "abandonment" of their country. But not many had such tragic family histories of political and personal persecution as the young Conrad — or such a legacy of patriotic obligations.

Furthermore, those who have contested the theory of Conrad's guilt complex were concerned only with the fact of his having left Poland as a young man. They did not take into account the much more serious matter of his choosing to write in a foreign language — and this at a time when the very survival of Poland was at stake, and when writers, more than anyone else, were needed to uphold the spirit of the nation. This, in the eyes of Conrad's fellow-countrymen, was the real desertion — a desertion harder to condone than the mere fact of his leaving his country.

The analogy of the beleaguered garrison, which I employed earlier, is meant to convey the attitude of Conrad's compatriots, and no doubt of Conrad himself, to the problem of patriotic responsibility.

Having said this, I can now turn to the main subject of this chapter. Every reader of Conrad must be struck by his obsession with the theme of desertion, betrayal and disloyalty, and the juxtaposed themes of fidelity to the bitter end and of unflinching dedication to one's duty.

One wonders whether, as some Conrad scholars have argued, the recurrence of these themes was due to a purely literary interest, or whether deeper motives, drawn from Conrad's own experience, were at work. This is, I think, a question that can only be answered by relating Conrad's books to his life. If we agree that the resemblances are significant, and that they recur with what looks like obsessive frequency, we shall feel entitled to claim that the result of the test is positive.

It is this test that I have carried out in the chapters that follow; and on their findings I feel justified in saying that a sense of guilt in relation to his own country — a sense of obligations neglected and of infidelity to the ideals of his dead parents — played a major part in his creative work.

For the reasons I have mentioned, scholars in Conrad's own country were the first to perceive, as early as 1920, when his books first appeared in Poland, the striking resemblances between the events described in his novels, and those in his own life. At the head of this group of Conrad scholars was a professor of Warsaw University, Józef Ujejski, whose book, *O Konradzie Korzeniowskim*,* remains a classic in this field.

My own interest in Conrad dates from about the time when translations of his works were becoming increasingly popular in Poland. I need hardly say that it never occurred to me that I myself might one day be a Conrad scholar. I started reading his books simply because other people were reading them. I did not, at first, even particularly like them. I came to them without any bias or preconceived opinion. I drifted through them with no special aim in mind. It was only when, in 1926, I read *The Rover* that I discovered the underlying symbolic meanings in them. I do not think that my discovery owed anything to outside influences. The idea that Conrad suffered from a sense of guilt towards his country suddenly struck me as a self-evident truth. I still have in my possession a draft of the essay on *The Rover* that I wrote at the time, and which I have incorporated in the chapter dealing with that book.

I have described the circumstances in which I first became acquainted with Conrad's writings because they have, to some extent, influenced the method I am now trying to apply to my readers. I want to lead them along the path that I took when I made my own discovery of the hidden aspects of Conrad's thought. I shall conduct them from one work to the next, pausing over each feature that may have some bearing on the final judgement. The method recalls that of a writer of detective stories, who sets the reader a problem, and then gradually allows him to uncover the mystery himself.

There is, however, a difference; unlike the detective-story writer, I hint at the solution right from the start. The reader will thus be able to check the validity of my arguments as he goes along.

I will now discuss the works of Conrad in turn, beginning with his second novel, *An Outcast of the Islands*.

* See Appendix, page 57.

56

Appendix

Stefan Zabierowski, in *Przegląd Humanistyczny* (No. 12, 1974 Warszawa), gives us more details on the subject of the reception of Conrad's books in Poland:

The early Polish interpretation of *Lord Jim* was based on the view that Conrad's novel is a kind of coded reply to the charge brought against him in Poland — the charge of "desertion"; of having sold his talent to foreigners.

The first person, I think, to suggest that *Lord Jim* had a symbolic meaning was Wiktor Gomulicki. In a review of *Lord Jim* entitled "Polak czy Anglik", ("A Pole or an Englishman"), Gomulicki wrote:

"This ship, doomed to sink; these travellers, overcome by sleep, and with nerves set on edge by religious ecstasy . . .; these egoists, whose desire for life drove them to escape from the ship that had been entrusted to them; above all, this essentially high-minded youth, quite out of place among those worthless men — this youth whose heart would be torn for the rest of his life, by the Promethean vulture of remorse; this "Lord" who later, in a foreign country, was to find prosperity, love and trust, and who would seek escape in a death he had deliberately courted. . . . Is all this, in its depths, only what it seems to an English reader? . . . Or is it a symbol?"*

Gomulicki's interpretation of Conrad's novel was echoed, with variations, by Wilam Horzyca, Stefan Żeromski, Maria Dąbrowska, Rafał Bluth and Józef Ujejski.

This deciphering of *Lord Jim* was often linked up with the interpretation given to Conrad's last novel, *The Rover*. But while *Lord Jim* was about "crime and punishment", *The Rover* was a symbolic rehabilitation of the author in relation to his country.

It was a Swiss scholar, Gustav Morf, the author of a book called *The Polish Heritage of Joseph Conrad* (1930), who carried the interpretation of *Lord Jim* even further, as a confession, in the form of a novel, of the author's guilt complex in relation to his country. To Morf, who analysed the novel by the methods of Freud's and Jung's depth psychology, *Lord Jim* was fundamentally symbolic.

The circumstances that led up to Jim's famous "leap" from the steamer *Patna* recall the circumstances that led to Konrad Korzeniowski's becoming a British subject. Jim's youth, as described in the novel, is a disguised version of Conrad's. In spite of his good family background and careful upbringing, Jim "leaps". He probably would not have done so but for the Captain's urging him and Jim's own conviction that the ship was about to founder. According to Morf, Jim's leap was an allegorical representation of Conrad's action at a certain moment in his life. Even the names of the ship and the country sound alike, especially in Polish (Patna-Polska). Poland, after the defeat of the Rising in 1863, appeared to be doomed.

**Życie i Sztuka, No. 1, 1905.

This psychological — and specifically Polish — interpretation of *Lord Jim* had other arguments in its favour, which let to the conclusion that the hero of the book was not only a portrait of the author — a psychological portrait of a private individual called Józef Teodor Konrad Nałęcz-Korzeniowski — but also (and this was equally important) a portrayal of the psychological characteristics of a racial group — that of the Poles. We find assertions of this kind, not only in the works of Polish critics, but, even more strikingly, in those of non-Polish writers, such as the French critic G. Jean-Aubry (G. Jean Aubry, "La Pologne dans la vie at l'ceuvre de Joseph Conrad", *Pologne Littéraire*, VI, 15 May 1922, 2).

AN OUTCAST OF THE ISLANDS

It might seem that the problem — to which Conrad was to return so often — of disloyalty to his country — was first brought home to him by Orzeszkowa's letter, and was first dealt with in *Lord Jim*.

A careful reading of *An Outcast of the Islands* — one of the earliest of Conrad's books: in fact, his second — supports the view that the inner conflict which threw a shadow over his subsequent life and work began much earlier.

The story of how the book came to be written should put us on our guard. When Unwin, the publisher, accepted Conrad's first novel, Conrad said to Garnett, who, as reader to the firm, had written an enthusiastic report on the book, "I don't expect to write again". According to what he said later, he only changed his mind when Garnett, choosing his words carefully, replied, "You have written one book . . . Why not write another?"* Conrad tells us, in his "Author's Note", that if Garnett had asked him why he should not "go on writing", he would have frighted him off writing for ever.

From Conrad's letters to his aunt Poradowska, we know that at the very time when he was announcing his intention of giving up writing, the idea of *An Outcast* was in his head, and the beginning of it was already on paper. How are we to account for his concealment of the truth and vehement denial? Was the vehemence a sign of inner conflict? There must have been some force at work to discourage him from further writing. But what force? In the "Author's Note", Conrad puts his resistance down to his loyalty to the sea and his reluctance to give up a seaman's life — a somewhat unconvincing argument. It is possible, as we know from the history

---

* *An Outcast of the Islands, p. VIII.*

of *Almayer's Folly*, to write novels even while one is at sea. We must look elsewhere for an explanation. The simplest that occurs to us is that Conrad already realised — or at least suspected — that although the one novel he had so far written in English, in his spare time, and probably without any thought of publication, did not commit him to becoming an English writer; a second would point to a deliberate decision on his part to devote his life to English writing. In his introduction to a book of Conrad's letters, Garnett thus describes the attitude of his new acquaintance before he started work on *An Outcast*:

"Of himself Conrad spoke as a man lying under a slight stigma among his compatriots for having expatriated himself. The subject of Poland was then visibly painful to him, and in those early years he would speak of it unwillingly, his attitude being designed to warn off acquaintances from pressing on a painful nerve".*

We should also remember that only a few years before this, Conrad had visited Poland for the first time after leaving it as a boy, and we may suspect that not all the memories left by this visit were pleasant.

It may well be that these memories lay behind Conrad's resistance to, and temporary rejection of a literary career. Even when he had written a second novel, he seemed rather displeased with himself for writing it; he said in the "Author's Note", "The story was never very near my heart".** Of no other work of his did he write with such dislike (see his letter dated 28. 10. 1895 to Edward Noble)*** — a dislike that there is nothing in the novel to justify. Such is sometimes the attitude of parents to a child whom they did not want.

The above argument is, of course based on mere supposition; to what extent it is justified, my further analysis of the novel will show.

The essential theme of *An Outcast* is the tragedy of betrayal and isolation. A white man breaks away from his own race by handing over to the natives the trading secrets of his friend and patron. But he cannot continue in his treachery; he cannot endure the loneliness among strangers or the isolation from his own people to which his disloyalty has condemned him. Even his love for a native woman — the love which prompted his treacherous act — turns to bitter hatred. Treachery brings its own punishment. Such is a brief summary of the inner meaning of the novel.

---

* E. Garnett, *Letters from Joseph Conrad 1895-1924*, Indianapolis, 1928, p. 6
** *An Outcast of the Islands*, p. IX.
*** Privately printed, 1925.

60

The second theme, which completes the first, is that of the curse inherent in the initial misdeed — the apparently unimportant false step which led on irrevocably to the next, more serious, transgression.

It is surely striking that when the author took the decisive step of separating himself from his own people by the final choice of a foreign language as a literary medium — that precisely *then* there should occur to him, as the subject of a novel, isolation from one's natural background, and the betrayal of one's race.

We are also struck by the way in which Conrad — who, in *Lord Jim*, "Karain" and *The Rescue*, describes, with unequalled mastery, the brotherly feeling that can exist between a white man and a coloured one — here stresses the unbridgeable gulf between the two races. The whole story of Willems is built up around this theme — his first instinctive repulsion against the idea of allying himself with a native woman, his inability to strike roots in his new surroundings, and, finally, his despairing solitude and downfall in a world wholly alien to him. The theme is hammered home relentlessly in all the decisive scenes of the book.

Most striking of all, however, is the fact that in no other book of Conrad's does the plot so clearly and unequivocally resemble his own problem. We have not here, as elsewhere, symbols and resemblances — the leap from the ship in *Lord Jim*, the abandonment of a brother in need in "The Lagoon", or the betrayal of a colleague in *Under Western Eyes*. Here the treachery is, quite simply, treachery to one's own race by a decision to transfer one's services to the people of another.

Let us consider the very first sentence of the novel. "When he stepped off the straight and narrow path of his peculiar honesty, it was with an inward assertion of unflinching resolve to fall back again into the monotonous but safe stride of virtue as soon as his little excursion into the wayside quagmires had produced the desired effect."* We cannot resist the suspicion that the words were inspired by the author's disquieting sense of his own situation, and that they convey, not only the idea of Willems' precarious position, but that of Conrad when he began to write the novel. It is worth noting that Willems' downfall took place in two stages. There was first the stage of dishonesty over business matters, and, later, as the inescapable consequence of his first wrongdoing, a much more serious action, which left a lasting stain on him — his betrayal of the white race.

---

* *An Outcast of the Islands*, p. 3.

When Conrad left Poland, his action also was in two stages — first, the harmless going to sea, and, later, his decision to devote his life to a literature that was not that of Poland.

To these simple and obvious analogies between Conrad's situation and the subject of his novel may be added a number of more subtle resemblances, which, taken singly, do not amount to much, but the sum of which has the force of proof.

Among the most interesting of these details is the name — Aissa — of Willems' Malayan mistress. When Conrad started writing *An Outcast*, he had not only decided to make his career as an English novelist, but to ally himself by marriage with an English wife — Jessie George — whom he had met in the same year (1894) at the house of his friends, the Hopes. Jessie... Aissa... was the extraordinary resemblance between the two names a mere coincidence? We know the tricks the subconscious can play.

In the novel, Aissa wants to detach her lover from his past — to make it impossible for him to return to his own people, and to keep him with her for life. Was Conrad afraid that this was just what Jessie would do, and may not this subconscious fear have expressed itself in his choice of the heroine's name? A psycho-analytical curiosity of this sort cannot, of course, be regarded as proof. But it is suggestive.

Another indication of the personal element in *An Outcast* is the fact that it contains certain themes which recur in Conrad's later work.

Thus a number of motifs found in *An Outcast* reappear in *Lord Jim*. Willems' reluctance to fight Lingard recalls Jim's refusal—born of his sense of guilt after Dain Warris's death—to defend himself. Even Lingard's narrow, self-confident morality in *An Outcast* is a somewhat ironic parallel to Captain Brierly's attitude to Jim's lapse. Aissa, in her anxiety both to detach and to shield her lover from the hostile world from which he came, at once reminds us of Jim's mistress, Jewel.

No less striking are the resemblances between *An Outcast* and another deeply personal story by Conrad — "Amy Foster". Willems' monologues in a language incomprehensible to poor Aissa are the prototype of Yanko Gooral's ravings, which drove his terrified wife out of the house. *An Outcast*, like "Amy Foster", is altogether a tragedy of the misunderstandings that take place between people of different cultures — of the inability of those living even in close proximity to know one another — of the total isolation of every human being. Willems and Aissa — white and brown — live and work, side by side, as strangers to each other, serving different ends and understanding no one but themselves.

Another of these recurring themes — indeed, the dominant one — is the theme of betrayal, which later appeared in so many of Conrad's finest works. In his Introduction to *Tales of Unrest* we find confirmation of his profound interest in the subject at the very time when he was writing *An Outcast*. He says that "The Lagoon", another story of treachery, was written immediately after he had finished *An Outcast*, and was "told in the same breath . . ., seen in the same vision, rendered in the same method". Moreover, Conrad points out in this Introduction how close the link is between "The Lagoon" and "Karain" — another story of betrayal, whose theme, he says, is almost identical with that of "The Lagoon".* The problem of treachery must, at that time, have taken an almost unbelievably strong hold on Conrad's mind. He could not shake off the obsession, even after he had dealt with it in *An Outcast*.

There seems to be only one argument against a subjective interpretation of *An Outcast*, and that is the complete objectivity with which (except for the last few chapters) it is written. Could anyone write quite so dispassionately about something in which he himself was involved? The whole problem, and all the characters (including even Captain Lingard, Conrad's beloved hero) are treated coolly, critically, almost slightingly. The moral judgement of Willems' action is simple and unambiguous, without emotional undertones or any of the bitterness or justifications that are so noticeable in *Lord Jim*. The question of betrayal seems to be kept a sword's length away from the author's soul. The tone of *An Outcast* is for Conrad so unusual as to be almost startling; but we should not let this mislead us. There may be various explanations of the fact that his first treatment of his own "desertion" of Poland was so unconcerned. We should remember that Orzeszkowa's letter had not yet been written; that no one had so far openly charged him with betrayal; and that he had not yet learnt, as Jim learnt, to hear its name in every whispered conversation. Thus it is quite possible that Conrad did not, at that time, identify Willems' case with his own. On 24th September 1895, when the first draft of the novel was finished, Conrad wrote to Garnett, who had advised certain alterations in it: "Nothing now can unmake my mistake . . .

---

* This, of course, is not the end of the list. I mention only those stories of betrayal which followed closely on the writing of *An Outcast*.

all my work is produced unconsciously (so to speak) and I cannot meddle to any purpose with what is within myself . . . it isn't in me to improve what has got itself written". The figure of the despised outcast, branded as a traitor, was suggested to him, as he tells us in the "Author's Note", by some memory of his Malayan experiences — a memory revived, perhaps subconsciously, by his own fears and remorse. The theme, however, at that stage, lived its own apparently separate life, and lent itself, as it was never to lend itself again, to objective treatment. This attitude must have gradually changed as the author mused over the fate of his un-heroic hero and entered more deeply into his drama. The last chapters of *An Outcast* — that nightmare of Willems' loneliness, when Lingard has cast him off and left him to the surrounding wilderness — give one the feeling that some dam had suddenly burst in Conrad's soul. The final pathos and tragedy of Willems' punishment outweigh the restrained and slightly disdainful tone of the beginning. The novel cannot, of course, tell us when, and to what extent, the author realised the analogy between his own drama and the one he was describing — nor is this question important. It is enough that we have grounds for supposing that in Willems' story Conrad is more or less consciously giving utterance to his own forebodings and fears, which we can still trace in the pages of this early novel.

This does not, however, explain the almost scornful note in the objectivity of *An Outcast*, and the disparagement of all the characters and affairs that come into it: but here again we must not allow ourselves to be misled. Willems' story may have taken the inglorious form it did take in Conrad's imagination, simply that it might be as unlike — as remote from — his case as possible. It is a well-known device in creative writing for an author to have it out with himself, ridicule his own faults, and administer justice to the puppet — distorted caricature of himself — that he has made his whipping-boy. Willems was probably Conrad's puppet.

All this entitles us to think that before Conrad began *An Outcast*, and while he was writing it, his attitude may have under-gone certain changes. After finishing *Almayer's Folly*, he must have realised, or at least have had an uneasy feeling, that he had crossed the Rubicon beyond which there could be no return to Poland; and that he would never be able to explain his conduct to his compatriots. His inner conflict and confusion were aggravated by the knowledge that there might still be time to draw back and avoid the charge of desertion, if *Almayer's Folly* remained the single literary freak of a seaman.

This surely accounts for the resistance and evasions that preceded the writing of his next book. In his "Author's Note" to *An Outcast*, Conrad explained this resistance, to himself and his readers, by his feeling of loyalty to the sea, and his unwillingness to give it up for a literary career. But underlying all this there must have been a still more important conflict. Would it not have been possible, as I have already suggested, to solve the problem by a compromise? What, for instance, was there to prevent him from both writing and going to sea, or writing and breaking off for a time, when he found work on a ship? There certainly would not have been the bitterness and horror that there was in Willems' drama if, in addition to Conrad's sense of disloyalty to the sea, there had not been, at the back of his mind, the reproach of another and more serious disloyalty — disloyalty to his own country: and if these two nagging thoughts had not intermingled and half-concealed each other. Perhaps the reason for Conrad's clinging so desperately to the sea was because it represented the one safe way out of his difficulty — the one way that would automatically put an end to the moral threat involved in life on land and a literary career. But he did, after all, write a second novel. He had been, no doubt, under considerable pressure, which helped to overcome his resistance. He makes it clear that Willems' boredom and sense of aimlessness on the alien and barbaric coast of Sambir, on which he had been abandoned, were the indirect cause of his falling head over ears in love with a girl — Aissa — whom he had met by chance. To Conrad, a seaman out of work and obliged to live on dry land, the fascination of writing a novel may have been as compelling as the love affair was for Willems — an enthralling form of escape from the dullness of life ashore. Moreover, the passion for writing aroused by his first novel was growing in him: and Garnett was urging him. Just at that time, too, Conrad's last strong link with Poland was broken by the death of his uncle, Tadeusz Bobrowski, who had been his counsellor, guardian and spiritual father. When old Lingard, who had looked after Willems from his boyhood, abandoned his unworthy charge to a life of solitude in a world of strangers, there may have been in this episode some memory of Conrad's uncle, going from him into the silence of death, just when his nephew had finished his first novel in English. There was no one now in his own country to whom he could speak of the decision that was to affect his whole life — no one to whom he had to account for his actions. He was living in a vacuum, which he had somehow to fill.

In the interval between finishing *Almayer's Folly* and beginning *An Outcast*, Conrad met his future wife, Jessie. This, no doubt, still further complicated his inner conflict, and finally brought it to a head. Conrad was now thinking, not only of adopting a foreign language, but of marrying a foreign woman — a twofold rejection of Poland: a twofold desertion. We know, from his letters to his uncle Bobrowski and his aunt Poradowska, that he had, for a long time, been feeling lonely and adrift — a mental state that he describes very penetratingly in the last chapters of *An Outcast*. He had searched desperately for some sustaining force, and hoped to find an aim and fulfilment in life through these two new bonds — a literary career, and marriage. But he was tormented by the feeling that they might only deepen his sense of solitude. He was afraid that, having broken irrevocably with those among whom he had been born, he was condemning himself to unceasing loneliness among people who perhaps could never understand him, and whom he himself might even come to hate, as Willems hated Aissa.

But the twofold spell of Jessie and the projected novel lured him by its promise to dispel the boredom and fill the void of his life — (as Willems hoped that Aissa's love would fill the emptiness of Sambir); at the same time, it provoked the spectre of a still more terrible void and of moral conflict. Does it not seem likely that this atmosphere called up the figure of Willems from the past, and helped to determine Conrad's future as a writer? All this, of course, is only a hypothesis. I do not think, however, that any other explanation would account equally well for the facts and mood connected with the writing of Conrad's second novel.

2.

It is, indeed, hard to understand why *An Outcast*, in spite of the light it throws on Conrad's own problems — to say nothing of its (no doubt more easily discernible) intellectual and artistic merits — was, from the first, the Cinderella of his work. Although H. G. Wells gave it a warm reception, it was for many years generally regarded as unsuccessful and second-rate, and in any discussion of Conrad's writings was dismissed with a brief notice. And, as we have seen, the author himself did not regard it with much favour.

It was only in the 1950's that reassessments of the book began to appear. In *The Kenyon Review* of 1953 a young American critic, Vernon Young, gave it a very fair appraisal, and in Poland Zdzisław Najder, in the new edition of the novel (1956), spoke of the "marks of greatness in this apparently feeble work". Young's opinion is worth quoting in full:

"*An Outcast of the Islands* consolidates features merely traced in *Almayer's Folly*. It is, by contrast, an achieved novel and better,I think, than most critics (and Conrad himself) have given it credit for being. It is dramatic in structure, cyclical in form; this is to say it proceeds narrative-wise by *progression d'effet* and its linear divisions are subsumed under a permeating motif. All the characters are logically disposed, developed and accounted for, while Willems is never superseded as the novel's leading character. The attentive reader of Conrad's work will find much to treasure in this early novel".*

I read Young's opinion with great satisfaction, for I myself have long had a high opinion of *An Outcast*, and have never been able to understand how its great and obvious merits came to be overlooked. The novel has, of course, many of the defects of literary inexperience — the thinness and unreality of the love scenes, the overdone parallels between the moods of nature and of man, and the intolerable wordiness of the descriptions. The author destroys the effect of even his best-drawn pictures by an accumulation of detail and metaphors, as though he never knew when to stop. It is not, however, the defects that should surprise us, but the general excellence of so early a book. If the clumsy *Almayer's Folly* meets with such favour, why not *An Outcast*?

Young drew attention to the book's technical merits — careful structure, the skilful manipulation of the characters, and, one may add, the ingenuity and convincing quality of the dramatic development of the plot. In what was only the second novel of an ex-sailor, one can only attribute such things to inspiration — a sudden blaze of artistic intuition.

These purely formal merits are, moreover, the least important of those that the novel has to give us. Its content is even more striking than its form. Above all, Conrad here showed, for the first time, his astonishing power of psychological analysis. Not only Willems, but all the characters — with the possible exception of Aissa — are seen to their very depths, and described in a few masterly words. It is this "psychological excellence" of the book that Najder stresses. Here

---

* Vernon Young: "Lingard's Folly: the Lost Subject", *Kenyon Review*, Autumn 1953.

too, for the first time, in Conrad's parenthetic, perceptive, and usually ironic remarks, he expresses the wisdom which, in a deepened form, is later to speak through Marlow. The Conrad who, in *Almayer's Folly*, was still the faithful disciple of Flaubert, boldly threw off, in *An Outcast*, his discipline of artistic discretion.

This overflowing abundance — now, for the first time, so sweeping and sure of its power — is the true mark of *An Outcast* in all its aspects. Young, for instance, points out that in the intrigues of the local people anxious to end Lingard's trading monopoly in Sambir, we have the first foreshadowing of the "material interests" in *Nostromo*. The rich diversity of the book — the socio-political structure underlying Willems' story — gives it the weight and solidity of life. This seems to me one of the most mature achievements of Conrad before he reached his full stature as an artist.

Finally, it is hard to resist a passing glance at the perfection of some of the passages in the novel. The last chapters, from the time of Willems' abandonment by Lingard, are the work of one who was already a master of emotional effects. The strangeness and horror of the hero's isolation, and the dramatic force (one has to admit, with a touch of melodrama) of the last chapter, are unforgettable.

The epilogue is brilliantly thought out: Willems' tragic story comes to us through the distorting mirror of an account given by two fools — Almayer and the drunken Rumanian. In this ironical summing-up we have yet another prototype of many of the endings of Conrad's books.

This particular ending is full of an almost metaphysical sadness. "The world's a swindle", cries out the drunken Almayer, and later on, an echo throws back mockingly his last word — "Hope".*

An Outcast is Conrad's first really pessimistic book. The sad mood of *Almayer's Folly* was sentimental and rather overdone. The pessimism of *An Outcast* is thought out, reasoned, and based on a hopeless view of life and the souls of men.

All the characters in the novel, even the best of them, are narrow, weak and slightly absurd. Even Lingard, with all his naive generosity, is made out to be a shallow simpleton. It is still, of course, a drama of individuals, but a drama already pervaded by the total tragedy of life — the senselessness of existence itself. The same mood, and an almost mature philosophical outlook, are reflected in the author's many asides scattered throughout the book. *An Outcast* already shows us the great Conrad; it is the first summit of his creative achievement.

And here I see one more — and this final — proof of my thesis.

_____
* *An Outcast of the Islands*, p. 367-8.

INITIATION INTO LORD JIM (I)

1. The Plot of *Lord Jim*

All literary criticism should start with a summary of the plot of the work under discussion, for one of the main functions of criticism is to isolate and clarify the central idea of the work. By ignoring the relatively unimportant and concentrating on the essential, a summary is in itself a kind of analysis.

In the case of *Lord Jim*, an analysis is particularly necessary. Jim's shifting fortunes are involved and confusing. Moreover, the author keeps changing, in no chronological order, from one narrator to another. And Marlow's comments, which crop up everywhere, do not always help one to understand the course of events — or at first sight do not appear to do so. A summary of the plot and of some of the more significant passages in the book at once shows that *Lord Jim* is not as obscure as it seems at first. The basic conception and idea of the book stand out clearly and simply, impressive in their depth and truth.

The summary falls into two parts — a brief outline of Jim's story, and a review of Marlow's comments.

I will begin with Jim's story — an analysis of his character and feelings.

Jim is an ambitious, highly imaginative and deeply sensitive young Englishman, who has brought with him from the country parsonage where his father was rector a fine tradition and all the marks of a good upbringing. But, being young, he sees life coloured by his imagination, and knows nothing of its dangers and pitfalls — nor, indeed, does he know much about himself. He enters the merchant navy in a mood typical of his character — dreaming of heroic exploits, and quite certain that he is capable of them and even marked out for them.

But during his training there occurs an incident which sounds a warning note, although Jim does not appear to realise its implications. During a storm, volunteers are needed to man a cutter that is going to the rescue of a small craft after a collision. Jim, half stunned by the fury of the storm, hangs back.

He loses his head in much the same way later, when, as an officer on an old steamer, the *Patna*, carrying pilgrims to Mecca, he is put to a far more serious test of character and seamanship. Real life turns out to be very different from his dream. When faced by a crisis, the ambitious Jim fails utterly.

The young officer of the *Patna* is partly responsible for the lives and safety of 800 people. What does he do when the ship hits a wreck, and threatens to sink at any moment? He does nothing. The over-active imagination to which he owes his love of adventure, and his sense of being pre-destined to deal with it, now appals him with a picture of inevitable catastrophe. He, who has dreamed of noble deeds, and been perpetually on the look-out for some great opportunity, finds his will paralysed when the opportunity arrives. He does not, indeed, think of escaping; he even stands ostentatiously apart when his colleagues, led by the captain, prepare to launch the lifeboat. But Jim never takes his eyes off it, and shows a suspicious interest in what the men are doing. His sense of honour is purely passive; he himself does not prepare the means of escape; he does not want to bear the responsibility for doing so; but he ends by making use of it. At the last moment, a sudden squall threatens to send the ship to the bottom. The members of the crew, escaping with the captain, shout out to a colleague on deck — not Jim, but a man who is in fact dead — to jump while there is still time. On a sudden impulse, it is Jim who jumps. What ought he to have done, if he had been more mature, and not a mere dreamer, full of good intentions but quite inexperienced? He would have done what every seaman in his position has done for centuries — let down all the lifeboats, packed into them as many people as they would hold, and been, himself, the last person to leave the ship.

In the lifeboat, Jim lives through the worst hours of his life. He is repelled by the wretched companions to whose level he has sunk, and so horrified by what he has done that he thinks of committing suicide.

The *Patna* does not sink. She is saved by a French gunboat, whose commanding officer, a model of seamanship, takes her in tow and stands on deck for hours, at the risk of his own life.

70

When Jim and his companions arrive in port, they are met by news of the *Patna's* rescue, and hear that they will have to face an enquiry for abandoning the ship in distress. Sooner than stand trial, the captain clears out. Jim stays where he is. He may, in a sudden crisis, have deserted his ship, but he is not going to deny his responsibility. He accepts it the more willingly because he feels that fate was, in a way, unjust to him, and that the blame was not only his, but lay to some extent in the appalling circumstances.

Jim may not have been justified in thus exonerating himself from an act implacably condemned by the simple moral code of the sea, but on the other hand his longing to convince himself of his innocence; his inability to accept his own weakness and disgrace; his belief, unshaken by this humiliating experience, in his ability to behave very differently — all this is an argument in his favour, the more so as he knows quite well how much to blame he really was, and is deeply ashamed of his conduct.

Such is the gist of the long talks between Jim and Captain Marlow, whom Jim meets by chance during the official enquiry. Marlow at once feels an interest in him, and has considerable sympathy with this mere boy who has been through so much. Marlow wants to help Jim, and even to arrange for him to slip away before the enquiry ends with the inevitable verdict of Guilty. Jim indignantly rejects Marlow's offer. "I mustn't shirk any of it", he says. What he has done, he must answer for. He wants to wipe the slate clean and, with undiminished resolution, to make a fresh start. The enquiry does, of course, find Jim guilty. He is deprived of his officer's rank, and his certificate is cancelled. Marlow comes to the rescue, and helps him to begin a new life by recommending him, as a friend, to a man he knows who can give him work. Jim is deeply touched and grateful. After the mishap of the *Patna*, he has begun to think that no one will ever trust him again. And trust is as necessary to him as the air he breathes.

Then an amazing thing happens. Jim does not, as many men would have done, go further downhill after the verdict. On the contrary, he carries out, in an exemplary manner, the fairly humble work that Marlow has found for him with a firm of ship-chandlers. Not only is he conscientious and hard-working, but he shows a degree of courage which, after the incident on the *Patna*, is hardly to be expected of him. He has risen above his downfall and disgrace with the extraordinary resilience that impressed Marlow from the start. Jim is consumed by a passionate desire for his own rehabilitation: he longs to redeem himself by hard work, and thus win back the respect he has lost. The very pain of his disgrace acts as a spur to him and prevents further lapses.

But his misdeed dogs him. Wherever he goes, people find out about his behaviour on the *Patna*. It is more than he can endure. He is over-sensitive to disgrace — even a past disgrace, for which his present honourable life has atoned. At any mention of what he did, he makes a scene, throwing over one job after another, and going off to increasingly remote places, where he will not be recognised. But for all his good intentions, the world seems to have no use for him. He is done for.

Marlow, however, shows himself a true friend. He never ceases to keep an eye on Jim. Once, when Jim has a terrible row with a sailor — as usual, over the *Patna* incident — and it looks as though he may never be offered work again, Marlow seeks the advice and help of a rich merchant and butterfly-collector, Stein. Stein, a man of great goodness and wisdom, at once shows extraordinary insight into Jim's over-emotional and ambitious nature, which he sees as the cause of all his failure, but as being at the same time the one hope for his future. Jim is a romantic, says Stein, adding, from his own experience — for he too is a romantic — that Jim cannot change, but must go his romantic way to the end. If he is to be helped, he must be given conditions in which he can demonstrate his full potential. His previous posts, hard though he worked in them, did not give him the incentive he needed, or the opportunity to achieve a lasting rehabilitation. He has to be completely detached from his past and sent into a new and distant world, where the work will be important enough to stimulate his ambition and imagination, and where other people will have enough faith in him to restore his self-confidence. "That", says Stein, "was the way. To follow the dream, and again to follow the dream — and so — *ewig* — *usque ad finem*..."* By this he seems to mean that if one is to achieve anything in life, one must aim high; that if, out of innumerable attempts that came to nothing, the romantic succeeds in only one, his life will find its fulfilment. But to abandon his dreams would inevitably lead to ultimate failure, to endless frustration, and to a deepening contempt for himself. Stein knows that the wisest thing one can do is to live in accordance with one's temperament — to be oneself.

Stein sends Jim as his agent to Patusan, an island almost entirely

* *Lord Jim*, p.214-5.

cut off from the outer world. His decision is a wise one. On Patusan, with its endless opportunities for helping a backward but trustful people that had known nothing but exploitation and oppression, Jim's great qualities, unrecognised or misunderstood by the world he has left, come into their own and are thereby strengthened. He is beginning to "master his fate".

But a great — surprisingly great — part of his success on Patusan is due to an unpremeditated act on his part — a leap which recalls the leap from the *Patna* that led to his undoing. With reckless courage, Jim has landed alone on Patusan, and at once been seized and put in a stockade by the despotic chief of the island, Rajah Allang. By the merest chance, Jim is not executed; he awaits his fate resignedly, with the indifference and lack of the instinct of self-preservation that are typical of a dreamer. It is not until the third day that he suddenly, for no particular reason, realises his danger, and, almost unthinkingly, decides to escape. He jumps — jumps over the stockade, as he jumped from the *Patna*. This time, he jumps to greatness. But what would have happened if he had landed in a swamp and been unable to scramble out — or if he had not at once met the friendly Doramin, Rajah Allang's enemy? So far, Jim's good fortune is undeserved, for he has neither planned nor worked for it.

Much the same thing happens later, when he is living with the half-cast, Cornelius. Here, too, Jim is almost entirely unconscious of the dangers surrounding him, and, but for the girl, Jewel, who is in love with him, protects and warns him, might not have left the house alive.

Largely due to the girl's help, Jim survives, and not only survives but defeats the ruffians set on him by Sherif Ali. By planning to defeat him, Jim takes his first decisive step towards gaining supremacy on Patusan.

His plan succeeds. With the help of Doramin's men, Jim crushes Sherif Ali and delivers Patusan from the dangerous scoundrel who had established a reign of terror all over the island. From that time onwards, Jim's prestige, fame and authority are unchallenged among the islanders, and far exceed his most sanguine expectations. He becomes the uncrowned king of Patusan. Rajah Allang is afraid of him; the inhabitants of Patusan, who regard him as their champion, worship him. He brings safety and prosperity to the island, establishes law and order, and feels responsible for every man, woman and child under his protection. The people have complete confidence in him, and treat his lightest word as a command.

Under the combined influence of success, the trust of other people, and his own increasing experience, he matures quickly, gaining strength and self-confidence, and coming very near to "mastering his fate". Now that circumstances are on his side, he shows that he can do more than dream of greatness — that he really is a remarkable man, and that the vague aspirations of his youth were not so far out. The undisciplined boy, ambitious, but without self-knowledge, has grown into a mature, strong man.

But his triumph on Patusan is not without its drop of bitterness. The same circumstances that led to Jim's success have certain aspects which cast a shadow over his happiness. The complete break with the past and his own people, the trust and devotion of the islanders that lay on him so heavy a burden of responsibility, the impossibility of entirely forgetting his past failure and disgrace, leave Jim only "nearly happy" in his new life. Even Jewel's love cannot dispel his deep sense of loneliness and of being misunderstood by those around him — a sense from which one is never completely free except in one's own country.

But as for returning to the world from which he fled and to which his feeling of guilt has barred the re-entry — this Jim does not want to do, and knows that he can never do. "Leave? For where? What for?", he asks Marlow during their last talk together. And he adds, "I shall be faithful", as though confining his faithfulness to the country where he is accepted, honoured and acknowledged.

Jim stays on Patusan, where, as he says, he is trusted. He has always needed the respect and trust of others, and the people of Patusan support and reassure him. He has not yet quite mastered his fate, for he is still too dependent on the trust of others, too much at the mercy of its fluctuations. It is a crisis of trust that leads to his tragic end.

Fate has one more ambush in store for him. A bandit called Brown, the head of a gang of cut-throats, lands on Patusan in search of food and anything else he can lay his hands on. He learns his mistake too late, when he finds himself surrounded by Doramin's men. Jim is away, and the people of Patusan wait for his return before dealing with the invader. So great is his authority that no decision is ever taken without him.

Jim returns and has a talk with Brown. Pity and a kind of rueful fellow-feeling for the man whom society has rejected, as it once rejected Jim himself, make him urge Doramin to release Brown

Conrad the sailor in 1883.

and his ruffianly gang. Doramin is reluctant to do so, but Jim carries his point at a council held by the elders of the tribe. The direct result of this decision is that Brown, when released, treacherously attacks and kills Dain Waris, Doramin's son and Jim's friend.

Jim has again failed those who trusted him, although this time there was no moral guilt in what he did. He does not, however, attempt to disclaim responsibility; come what may, he will not try to escape again. Face to face with the heartbroken Doramin, he will either regain his confidence or pay for the appalling blunder with his life — which, without the trust of others, is valueless to him. He stands before Doramin, and waits fearlessly while the grief-stricken father levels a pistol at him. He makes no effort to escape. He has risen to the heights of that heroism of which he has always dreamed. And he is killed. But he is victorious, for he stood his ground unflinchingly; in spite of his escape from the *Patna*, no one will ever dare to look down on him again.

2. Marlow's Comments

Apart from the narrative about Jim, almost a third of the book is made up of the comments and reflections of the narrator, his friend Marlow. Marlow's reflections are many — far more than are needed to throw light on Jim's story; they seem, indeed, to have a life of their own. For *Lord Jim* is a kind of dialogue — a symphony of two interweaving and complementary motifs — the motif of Jim himself, and that of his philosophising friend. To get the complete picture, the reader must take Marlow's comments separately, and discover their true meaning and purpose, and the part they play in the book.* What follows is a summary, composed chiefly of quotations, of the gradual development of Marlow's views on Jim.

1. When Marlow first saw Jim at the magistrate's court he immediately felt a great interest in him. Why? Marlow's first remarks (Chapter V) show that the sight of Jim undermined his own faith in man and set him mentally debating the whole concept of honourable behaviour, of which Jim seemed — alas, so misleadingly — to be the personification.

"He looked", says Marlow, "as genuine as a new sovereign, but

---

* The extracts from *Lord Jim* are given verbatim throughout. I have, however omitted some sentences which seemed relatively unimportant, and connected others which, although occuring separately, refer to the same subject.

there was some infernal alloy in his metal. How much? The least thing — the least drop of something rare and accursed; the least drop! But he made you — standing there with his don't care-a-hang air — he made you wonder whether per chance he were nothing more rare than brass."*

"Was it for my own sake that I wished to find some shadow of an excuse for that young fellow whom I had never seen before, but whose appearance alone added a touch of personal concern to the thoughts suggested by the knowledge of his weakness — made it a thing of mystery and terror — like a hint of a destructive fate ready for us all whose youth — in its day — had resembled his youth?."**

To Marlow, then, at this first encounter, all men are on trial with Jim, for Jim inspires confidence; he looks an honourable man. Moreover, he reminds Marlow of his own high-minded, idealistic youth. If a man like that lets one down, whom can one trust?

2. As he listens to Jim's long confession, full of evasions and half-truths, but full too, of noble illusions, a latent sense of guilt, and proud determination to accept full responsibility, Marlow's opinion of him changes (Chapter XI). He no longer feels only the doubt and scepticism of an older man. Jim's idealistic youthfulness begins to fascinate him, and to throw a softening light over the disastrous act he has committed. "A mysterious light seemed to show me his boyish head, as if in that moment the youth within him had, for a moment, gleamed and expired. . . . He was a youngster of the sort you like to see about you . . . of the sort whose appearance claims the fellowship of those illusions you had thought gone out, extinct, cold, and which, as if rekindled at the approach of another flame, give a flutter deep, deep down somewhere, give a flutter of light . . . of heat! . . . Yes; I had a glimpse of him then . . . and it was not the last of that kind . . ."***

3. Marlow's judgement of Jim begins to vacillate (Chapters XVI-XVIII). Belief alternates with doubt — and Jim's behaviour often justifies the doubt. Marlow does not find him easy to understand. There is something elusive about him.

When the court case is over, and Marlow has written his letter of recommendation, he is "almost alarmed" by Jim's transport of gratitude. Exaltation so often ends in disillusionment.

---

* *Lord Jim*, p. 45-6.
** Ibid., p. 51.
*** *Ibid.*, p. 128.

Jim leaves him. "But as to me, left alone with the solitary candle, I remained strangely unenlightened. I was no longer young enough to behold at every turn the magnificence that besets our insignificant footsteps in good and in evil." And then Marlow adds, expressing what has become his habitually ambivalent view of Jim, "it was yet he, of us two, who had the light."*

4. At Stein's (Chapter XX), Marlow is finally able to solve the problem of Jim. When Stein says that Jim is romantic, Marlow remarks, "He had diagnosed the case for me, and at first I was quite startled to find how simple it was."** For he now sees Jim's life as "rich in generous enthusiasms, in friendship, love, war — in all the exalted elements of romance."***

The fascination of Jim's personality is now complete. He emerges from shadow into radiant light. The defendant almost turns into the judge, who is in possession of the truth — perhaps of absolute truth. "His imperishable reality came to me with a convincing, with an irresistible force! I saw it vividly, as though . . . we had approached nearer to absolute Truth, which, like Beauty itself, floats elusive, obscure, half submerged, in the silent still waters of mystery."**** "For", says Marlow elsewhere, "it was . . . like all our illusions, which I suspect to be only visions of remote, unattainable truth, seen dimly."*****

5. The shadow, of course, returns. The experienced and self-disciplined Marlow cannot, after all, entirely understand Jim's impulsive and undisciplined youth. Marlow never quite knows what to make of it. Before Jim leaves for Patusan (Chapters XXII-XXIII), Marlow is again besieged by doubt. "He impressed, almost frightened, me with his elated rattle . . . Such an attitude of mind in a grown man and in this connection had in it something phenomenal, a little mad, dangerous, unsafe . . . It was the same mood, the same and different, like a fickle companion that today guiding you on the true path, with the same eyes, the same step, the same impulse, tomorrow will lead you hopelessly astray . . . Strange, this fatality that would cast the complexion of flight upon all his acts, of impulsive, unreflecting desertion — of a jump into the unknown. It is precisely the casualness of it that strikes me most . . . I am fated never to see him clearly," says Marlow finally.******

---

* Lord Jim., pp. 185-6.
** Ibid., p. 212.
*** Ibid., p. 217.
**** Ibid., p. 216.
***** Ibid., p. 323.
****** Ibid., pp. 234-241.

6. But Jim, in spite of everything, masters his fate. "It was something to be proud of", says Marlow, after his visit to Patusan (Chapter XXIV). "It was not so much of his fearlessness that I thought. It is strange how little account I took of it: as if it had been something too conventional to be at the root of the matter. No. I was more struck by the other gifts he had displayed. He had proved his grasp of the unfamiliar situation, his intellectual alertness in that field of thought . . . And all this has come to him in a manner like keen scent to a well-bred hound."* We are already close to the apotheosis of Jim. "I affirm he has achieved greatness," Marlow declares. And for the first time we hear him say, "Jim seemed to have come very near at last to mastering his fate."**

7. There is just one more apparent recurrence of Marlow's scepticism about Jim. When Marlow is talking of him to Jewel (Chapter XXXIII), he says with sudden bitterness that "the world did not want him," and, when asked why, replies, "because he is not good enough."*** But this outburst is not to be taken literally. We see later that what really called it forth was not a return of his doubts over Jim, but resentment against the world for not appreciating him.

8. Immediately after this outburst there comes what is perhaps the most penetrating explanation of Jim's fate (Chapter XXXIV). "For my part, I cannot say what I believed — indeed I don't know to this day, and never shall probably . . . There is a law, no doubt . . . It is not Justice the servant of men, but accident, hazard, Fortune — the ally of patient Time."****

This should probably be taken to mean that fate and chance may bring out precious qualities in men, but may, in other circumstances, destroy them, so that there can never be a wholly just judgement of anyone — too much depends on fate and luck. Fate has indeed overpowered Jim, but the same fate later led him to greatness.

This idea of Marlow's is, however, only one element in his final judgement. Fate decides many things. But fate ought to be mastered. Has Jim mastered it? Marlow is not sure.

9. But he is sure when Jim lies at Doramin's feet with a bullet through his heart. "Not in the wildest days of his boyish visions

---

* *Lord Jim,* p. 248.
** Ibid., p.274.
*** Ibid., p.318.
**** Ibid., p. 320.

could he have seen the alluring shape of such an extraordinary success! For it may very well be that in the short moment of his last proud and unflinching glance, he had beheld the face of that opportunity which, like an Eastern bride, had come veiled to his side . . . Is he satisfied — quite, now, I wonder? We ought to know. He is one of us — and have I not stood up once, like an evoked ghost, to answer for his eternal constancy? Was I so very wrong after all? Now he is no more, there are days when the reality of his existence comes to me with an immense, with an overwhelming force . . ."*

In this last colloquy with Jim's shade there is no longer any doubt — only deep respect and affection. There is, too, a feeling that the things that Jim stood for — love, loyalty, enthusiasm, a noble pride — are the only true and important values in life — values that may even be manifestations of absolute Truth. This is probably what Marlow has in mind when he speaks of the *reality* of Jim's existence.

3. The Idea in *Lord Jim*

All true works of art are, so to speak, autonomous; they have their own life and relative independence of their creator. This is true of *Lord Jim*, that drama of lost honour ending with the victory of the romantic ideal of conduct. We see the point of the story both from the plot, and from Marlow's reflections.

I now propose to discuss the underlying idea of the book from another angle, by seeing how the idea gradually took shape in the author's mind. The objective meaning of *Lord Jim* will gain added poignancy and depth from this analysis.

A comparison of Conrad's life with the plot of *Lord Jim*, has shown how profoundly personal the book is. Even its structure — the dialogue between Marlow and Jim — suggests that both men are embodiments of the author — the mature Conrad, disciplined by English ways, but disillusioned by life, and the young Conrad, boyish and unstable, but unquestionably richer in hope and noble ambition.

Many elements, no doubt, combined to form the plot of *Lord Jim*. The story may have been based on some real adventure at sea,

---

* *Lord Jim*, p. 416.

or some event in Conrad's life, in which he failed to live up to his own dreams. We at once recall the crisis in Marseilles, when Conrad, still very young, and having left Poland only a few years before, came to grief over his irresponsible handling of his uncle's money.* By so doing, he lost the confidence of his uncle Bobrowski and, like Jim in other circumstances, only regained it by long and arduous service in the British Merchant Navy until, finally, he triumphed.

This experience may have been the germ of the short story which he later expanded into the novel about Jim. But there are no available data to tell us what made Conrad expand and develop his first rather sketchy idea. This is a mystery on which I hope to throw some light.

As I see it, the Marseilles crisis, nobly atoned for by Conrad's subsequent conduct, and in any case a thing of the past, could not have called forth so passionate and personally involved a trial as that which Conrad held on Jim. Some very powerful factor must have been at work just at the time when Conrad was writing *Lord Jim*. I myself have sufficient reasons to think that the inspiration of the whole novel as it finally developed was the problem familiar to us from his life — the problem connected with his leaving his oppressed country and thereby laying himself open to a charge of desertion.

We also know that what brought the matter to a head may have been Orzeszkowa's article, which, as we remember appeared at about the time when Conrad had written the first few pages of the story. In all probability then, *Lord Jim* was a conscious or sub-conscious reply to Orzeszkowa's accusation: and, even more, it was an inner debate between the author and his conscience. It goes without saying that what hurt him most was not the accusation itself, which he could have dismissed as slander, but the very existence of the problem, of which he must have been aware long before the article was written — at least from the time when his

---

* Every young man goes through a period of irresponsibility, during which he sows his wild oats. But there was a special bitterness in Conrad's failure. When he left Poland, against the wishes of his family and even at the risk of being thought disloyal to his country, he knew that his ambition would make exacting demands on him; it was up to him to prove that he had acted rightly, and that his apparent abandonment of Poland was justified by what he achieved. But his three years in Marseilles seemed to show the exact opposite — that not only had he failed to achieve anything, but that he was up to his ears in debt. The Marseilles failure must have been far more bitter to him than such escapades usually are to the young scape-graces involved in them, and was no doubt the reason for his suddenly changing his whole way of life.

first book was published in English. The article only precipitated the crisis. It changed a mere literary idea of a sea-story into a probing self-analysis that went far deeper than the accusation itself, and grew, as Conrad went on writing, into the anguish of Jim's fundamental question: What am I worth?

Conrad seems, in the novel, to put himself in the dock, asking if he is to blame, and ready, like Jim at the enquiry, to take the responsibility for his own "escape" from Poland, and the way of life he has since chosen. Let us look at this symbolic trial.

First we shall have to establish what analogies, if any, exist between Jim's guilt and that of his creator. There are, of course, considerable differences between the two cases. Conrad was only concerned with the fact of Jim's guilt and the effect of this guilt on his conscience; there was no real similarity between the *Patna* episode and Conrad's abandonment of his country. It was neither fear nor the instinct of self-preservation that drove him out into the world, but the love of adventure; his motive was positive, not negative. His guilt was more complex and subtle than Jim's. Nevertheless, the main theme of *Lord Jim* is a youth's dream of heroism — ending in flight.

Was not this to some extent Conrad's problem too? Jim fled; Conrad — left. For both it became a moral issue — for Jim, an obvious one; for Conrad, a hidden crisis that only slowly emerged into his consciousness. Both Jim and Conrad had to face the damning verdict of public opinion, although in different degrees and different circumstances. Jim's final rehabilitation on Patusan reminds us of another island — England and Conrad's final literary triumph. In view of all this, we are surely justified in regarding *Lord Jim* as an exposition of Conrad's own problem.

Let us now consider the question of Jim's guilt, and assess the results of our enquiry. What first strikes us is the unusually detailed analysis of Jim's emotional and mental condition before his escape from the supposedly sinking ship. It is obvious that Conrad tries to pierce to the very heart of Jim's guilt, as though he were personally involved in it, as Marlow, his *porte-parole*, really is. Jim's was not an ordinary flight, and the verdict cannot be ordinary either.

According to maritime law, he was undoubtedly guilty. Conrad is, however, obviously at great pains to show how complex such things can be. It was Jim's duty to save as many people as he could, and to be the last into the lifeboat, instead of suddenly panicking and following his companions' cowardly example. He, who had entered the merchant navy with such high ideals, should, of all men, have observed the seaman's simple code of behaviour.

Nor is it only a question of Jim's flight from the *Patna*. He is altogether unstable and unpredictable, up to the time of his life on Patusan, where he at last achieves maturity; but almost to the end Marlow, in spite of his sympathy and admiration for Jim's good qualities, cannot help wondering whether there is any guarantee that he will not again do something disastrous — whether, in fact, he can be trusted.

There are, of course, extenuating circumstances. Jim is still young and inexperienced when he is put to a very severe test. He is not at heart a coward, or a man to whom duty means nothing; it is his over-active imagination that numbs him and paralyses his will by conjuring up a picture of inevitable disaster. And the imagination which shows him the impossibility of saving all the passengers blinds him to the fact that he might at least save some. Jim jumps into the lifeboat on an impulse, just as on Patusan he will again save his life by following another impulse. Moreover, sensitive as he is to the opinion of others, he has to face his test without the awareness that people whom he respects are watching him, and without any example that could give him courage. He has no one on the vast sea to rely on but himself.

In Conrad's flight from Poland, we find almost the same extenuating circumstances — youth, immaturity, the power of a vivid imagination, the unpredictable impulse; and, finally, the lack of support given by the knowledge that one's own people are looking on while one is taking some momentous decision. In later life, too, Conrad explained many things — above all, his choice of a literary career — by the unpredictability of his impulses.

More important than all else, however, is the fact that Jim, in spite of what he has done, is still fundamentally honest. He is to blame, but he wants to pay the price, to shoulder the responsibility. He makes no attempt to evade the enquiry.

Above all, he wants to restore his good name. And he can do it. Notwithstanding his bitter experience, he secretly believes in himself, and cannot bear a life of disgrace. His disastrous act is not final — on the contrary, it spurs him on to start again and to become a stronger and better man.

The personalities and comments of Captain Brierly and the officer of the French gunboat help us to form our judgement. Jim's action and attitude, when compared with theirs, are seen in perspective. Brierly, a puritanical Englishman, and something of a caricature (a fact which shows us that Conrad's sympathies are not on his side), is self-confident and priggish, dogmatic, unbending, and with only a narrow-minded concept of duty. When, to his great astonishment, he gets into serious trouble and breaks under the strain, he can see only one way out — to give up his job and his life. Conrad does not seem to think that this is the most difficult way out a man can chose.

Conrad is, perhaps, most impressed by the Frenchman, who is experienced and compassionate, with no illusions concerning the weaknesses of human nature. Nevertheless, his view is that one should hold out to the end, and that honour must come first.

Jim stands midway between the two men. He believes, unreflectingly, in himself, and is buoyed up by ambitions and hopes, for which at present there appears to be no justification. He lacks the critical spirit and self-knowledge of the Frenchman, but is less superficial and more resilient than Brierly; being, moreover, without the discouragement of too clear an insight into himself, he continues to believe in his hidden merits. After his fall, he acquires greater depth and self-knowledge, and does not try to find an easy way out of life, but wants honestly to atone; and in the end he triumphs.

Thus Conrad, a just judge, sitting in symbolic judgement on himself, admits his own weakness and guilt, and cannot even guarantee a future free from error. Even when Marlow speaks of Jim positively, Conrad usually qualifies his remarks by adding a dubious "it seems", "almost", "surely", as though to stress the objective caution with which he regards the matter. On the other hand, he says that in such circumstances it is all too easy for a young man to do the wrong thing. Moreover, he stresses that there is a great deal of good in Jim, who becomes stronger and more entitled to respect after the disaster than he was before.

This, however, is not all. The judgement incurred by a youthful error is not the only theme in the book. It is only the starting-point. Conrad goes further, passing from the problem of guilt to the whole question of the romantic attitude to life, and unexpectedly decreeing that the unstable Jim, now in the dock, shall rise to greatness.

When one theme ousts another in an author's work, we should always look for his motive. An artist is an architect; when he changes his original design, he does so for some very good reason — or, if he is swayed by a sudden impulse, this too is the expression of a hidden purpose. What was in Conrad's mind? Let us try to find out.

In the analysis of Jim's wrongdoings, his youth is accountable for much. It is both an extenuating and an incriminating circumstance. For quite a long time, Marlow feels that he cannot trust this undisciplined and highflown youthfulness: it seems too unpredictable. And, while he sees the charm of youth, he is put off by its instability and the contrast between its lofty aims and poor performance. In this startling discrepancy Marlow sees the weakness and failure of mankind in general. His attitude at the beginning is expressed in the words "Hang ideas!", for ideas only confuse the simple sense of duty.

But as he sees more of Jim's essentially noble nature, his attitude changes. Youth is, indeed, unreliable, but it is courageous and spiritually rich, and it aims high. It has within it latent possibilities which, as one grows older, fade away or are forgotten. It is the true springtime of life, when everything that is most precious in the soul — however unfitted to stern reality it may be — breaks into exuberant growth. In what is the turning-point of the book — Marlow's talk with Stein — the obsessive daydreaming that counted for so much in Jim's blunder, and which Marlow dismisses with the words "Hang ideas!", is not only exonerated but raised to a supreme value. Jim's wrong action was, indeed, born of his dream, but, to a romantic like himself, there is nothing for it but "to follow the dream, and again to follow the dream" — to err, but perhaps at last to achieve some high aim in life. In the blunders and fine qualities of Jim's youth, Stein discerns his romantic nature; and it is this that completely changes Marlow's attitude. The theme of vacillating and unreliable youth almost disappears from the book, and its place is taken by the noble theme of romanticism. Jim, its personification, overcomes his evil destiny. We must, then, learn to take a different view of youth, and of romanticism which is another name for it. We must recognise the nobility of this attitude to life, and, if we have to sit in judgement on its failures, we should do so cautiously and tenderly, for perhaps it is this attitude, and not our own, that "has the light and truth".

Now we begin to discover what Conrad had in mind. While writing the book, he was probably making the same mental and emotional journey as Marlow — but making it with reference to himself. He too, musing over the youth charged with so heavy a burden of guilt, must have been fascinated and impressed by the beauty — the half-forgotten beauty — of youth itself, with its idealism and bold ambition. And, after the anguish of self-judgement, he must have experienced a proud reaction when he reflected that the dreamy boy who had uprooted himself from Poland in search of adventure was not, after all, the least worthy of men, and that all he had achieved over the years in an alien country — the status of a first-class seaman and later of a successful writer — showed that this boy had had in him the makings of a fine man, and had not wasted the talents given to him. Above all, and in spite of all, there had been some meaning, some guiding line in that erring and tragic life; and this line was to be found precisely in the romanticism of youth, in the relentless pursuit of youth's lofty dreams. This vivid awareness of a truth which he had, perhaps, always known, but had only dimly perceived, must have seemed to him like a firm path under his feet after he had struggled out of a swamp. Then, too, at the decisive twist of the novel, he may have suddenly realised — or just intuitively felt — that the best way of defending one's chosen path in life is not by trying to explain away the mistakes common to us all, but by revealing the significance of this path, and pointing to the goal which is its final justification.

To this we owe, no doubt, the note of deep sincerity and the pathos of expression that Conrad brought to the second part of the book, which is the vindication and fulfilment of Jim's romantic attitude to life. And the same explanation accounts for Conrad's deep understanding and convincing interpretation of a subject as often misrepresented, and therefore as suspect, as romanticism. In the spiritual life of Conrad, the sailor and poet, the "romantic attitude to reality" was always the essential element. But after Orzeszkowa's accusation, this romantic attitude had become the *raison d'être* — the full explanation and justification — of everything in that life. One detail will show us how much love, faith and hope Conrad put into his glorification of the romanticism that Jim personified. Conrad's tragic life had not inspired him with faith in the metaphysical purpose of existence. The only one of his books in which he seems to discern, through the noble figure of its hero, "the absolute truth, half submerged in the silent waters of mystery", is, precisely, *Lord Jim*. The fact that Conrad, the confirmed pessimist, tries by this argument, rare in his work, to account for the Jims of this world, has its own eloquence and significance.

Thus, in spite of everything, there is a note of muted triumph in *Lord Jim* — that dialogue between the negative and positive aspects of Conrad's own life — a dialogue in which the disturbing voice of conscience is met by the sense of being essentially in the right.

*   *   *

Some readers may think me arbitrary in thus interpreting the themes in *Lord Jim* as a symbolical representation of the author's own problems. I would remind such readers of a few passages in the book, in which Conrad abandons the fictional framework, drops the disguise of the symbol, and seems to speak, in his own voice, of the country and people he had left behind.

1. Here, for instance, is what Marlow says, before leaving Jim in Patusan, about returning to one's own country (Chapter XXI): " . . . it seems to me that for each of us going home must be like going to render an account. We return to face our superiors, our kindred, our friends — those whom we obey, and those whom we love; but even they who have neither, the most free, lonely, irresponsible, and bereft of ties, — even those for whom home holds no dear face, no familiar voice, — even they have to meet the spirit that dwells within the land, under its sky, in its air, in its valleys, and on its rises, in its fields, in its waters and its trees — a mute friend, judge, and inspirer. Say what you like, to get its joy, to breathe its peace, to face its truth, one must return with a clear consciousness. All this may seem to you sheer sentimentalism . . . But the fact remains that you must touch your reward with clean hands."*

2. Of his stay on Patusan, Jim says (Chapter XXXII): "I've been only two years here, and now, upon my word, I can't conceive being able to live anywhere else. The very thought of the world outside is enough to give me a fright; because, don't you see . . . I have not forgotten why I came here. Not yet! . . . If such a thing can be forgotten, then I think I have a right to dismiss it from my mind . . . Is is not strange that all these people who would do anything for me can never be made to understand? They can never know the real, real truth . . . never! I talk about being done with it — with the bally thing at the back of my head . . . Forgetting . . . Hang me if I know!"**

---

* *Lord Jim* pp. 221-2.
** Ibid., pp. 305-6.

3. Marlow's conversation with Jewel, on the subject of Jim, is of exceptional interest (Chapter XXXIII). To calm her down in Jim's absence, Marlow speaks with a concentrated passion unique in the novel — a passion unintelligible unless one assumes that Marlow's words are an outburst from the writer himself. "What I had to tell her was that in the whole world there was no one who ever would need his heart, his mind, his hand... From all the multitudes that peopled the vastness of that unknown there would come, I assured her, as long as he lived, neither a call nor a sign for him. Never. I was carried away. Never! Never! I remember with wonder the sort of dogged fierceness I displayed."***

4. Before leaving Patusan, Marlow says to Jim (Chapter XXXV), "You have had your opportunity."... "Had I?" — he said. — "Well, yes. I suppose so. Yes. I have got back my confidence in myself — a good name — yet sometimes I wish... No! I shall hold what I've got. Can't expect anything more." He flung his arm out towards the sea. "Not out there anyhow... This is my limit, because nothing less will do... Will you be going home again soon?" "In a year or so if I live."... "Tell them..." he began... "No — nothing," — he said.'****

I have purposely made no comment on the passages quoted above. They speak for themselves. One has only to substitute Conrad for Jim, and for Patusan — England.

There is further evidence in support of my thesis that the story of *Lord Jim* had a personal background. This evidence is drawn from the various dates on which the book was started and restarted. Conrad wrote the first draft, dealing only with the incident of the *Patna*, in, aproximately, April 1898. There then followed a period of indecision, unsuccesful attempts to continue the story, and near despair over it. In April 1899, Orzeszkowa published her article, of which Conrad probably heard from friends in Poland in early June, or even May. In July of the same year he set to work at top speed on the rest of the novel, and did not stop until he had finished it. There were of course the usual breaks in writing, but the speed was unquestionable. What was the driving force behind this sudden outburst of creative energy after so long a period of frustration over the story? When one considers the dates, the answer seems obvious.

*** *Lord Jim*, p. 318.
**** Ibid., pp. 333-335.

INITIATION INTO *LORD JIM* (II)

1. *Lord Jim* as a work of art

It is not my purpose in this chapter to evaluate *Lord Jim* as a work of art. But a few words on this aspect of the book may not be out of place, since it is closely linked with my main theme.

It should be said at once that the artistry of the book is no less remarkable than the originality of its ideas and psychological analysis. *Lord Jim* has obvious structural defects, divided as it is into two parts — almost, one might say, two separate stories: one, the *Patna* case; the other, Jim's life on Patusan — differing from one another in mood, descriptive technique, psychological depth, and delicacy of finish. How is it that, in spite of these formal imperfections, the book succeeds in being such a fascinating work?

There can be no doubt that this uneven work contains the most interesting and original solution that Conrad ever found to the problem of fictional form. If, even today, the book arouses interest and admiration, the reason lies partly in its daring and very modern narrative technique.

The novelty of its approach (a truly astonishing novelty, at the time when the book was written) is largely due to the fact that the author's attitude to the hero is not that of the godlike omniscience ordinarily assumed by a novelist as he gradually reveals to the reader the truth that he himself has known from the start. Conrad's approach is far more personally involved, active, changeable — one may say, life-like (A. J. Guerard calls it impressionistic). The author, like the reader, seems to be only partly in the secret, and uncertain of the outcome; then, gradually together with the reader, he gets to know the hero and forms a moral judgement on him — as happens, in much the same way, in life itself.

A. J. Guerard, in his excellent study *Conrad the Novelist* has this to say: "*Lord Jim* appears at the turn of the century as the first novel in a new form: a form bent on involving and implicating the reader in a psycho-moral drama which has no easy solution; bent, too, on engaging his sensibilities more strenuously and even more uncomfortably than ever before. An essential novelty, although borrowed perhaps from the mystery or 'police' tale, is to force upon the reader an active, exploratory, organizing role."*

The reader who agrees with what I have been saying in the preceding chapters will accept the conclusion that Conrad probably hit upon this new and challenging form of presenting an enquiry into Jim's guilt and true worth simply because this was how he, when seeking his own truth, discovered it within himself. Was not Marlow's attitude to his hero — an alert, questioning attitude, that examined the facts from every angle without ever attaining final certitude — exactly the same?

The book is an interesting example of the fact that, in art, originality of idea and form is not usually the result of a deliberate attempt to find novel solutions to the problem of form; the new form appears spontaneously, so to speak, when the author has something really new and original to say. And, where the main theme discussed above, is concerned, an additional and unintentionally revealing confirmation of Conrad's deep personal involvement in Jim's drama may be found in this aspect of the book as a work of art.

2. Three Appendices

I want to conclude my study with two separate observations — one on the Polish features of Jim's temperament; the other on betrayal as a subject of special importance in the history of Poland under foreign oppression. I think that these two themes, although only loosely connected with the novel, may throw a good deal of light on its central problem. As my third contribution, I give the text of Orzeszkowa's article. There is also a postscript to the chapter.

A. Polish Connections

To English readers, Jim is a fascinating but somewhat enigmatic figure. They are baffled, as Marlow was at first, by this boy, so

---

* A. J. Guerard, *Conrad the Novelist*, Harvard University Press, Cambridge, Massachusetts, 1958, p. 126.

Conrad after finishing Nostromo *in 1904.*

clearly in the wrong when he fled from an apparently sinking ship, but who afterwards takes the matter to heart beyond all reason, and is unable to return to normal life. Then — amazingly, after this unpromising beginning — he turns into the heroic and mature ruler of Patusan.

To a Polish reader, the moral fluctuations of Jim's life present no problems; from first to last they are entirely comprehensible. For Jim, although nominally English, has the psychological characteristics of a Pole — as had his creator. For the English reader, some knowledge of the principal marks of the Polish character may, therefore, throw light on the book and its hero.

The Polish character may briefly be described as a mixture of extreme sensibility and vivid imagination, backed by unyielding ambition; the Poles are a proud race. The predominant feature of their character is, however, the diversity and incongruity of its elements. I will make my meaning clearer by arranging these elements in groups:

1. A dreamy and proud confidence in oneself and one's ability, alongside inconsistency and a lack of perseverance and an established standard of behaviour — a combination which often leads to crises and disillusionment. On the other hand — an unusual resilience, a passionate longing for rehabilitation, a proud refusal to accept any downfall as final, and the ability, after the most crushing defeat, to dash back into the fray and unexpectedly come out victorious. Polish history gives many examples of this.

2. Great sensitiveness to the judgement and opinions of other people; a longing to be trusted, respected and admired — and, in consequence, a tendency to be unduly affected by what others are thinking. But, on the other hand, a simultaneous wish to distinguish oneself and show one's best side to the world. Finally, in spite of this excessive preoccupation with human opinion, a strong individualism and a determination to have one's own way, combined with an ardent love of independence and freedom.

3. A disquieting tendency to let one's energy and productive activity depend on some outward incentive. In everyday life, when an adequate incentive is lacking, even the most characteristic good qualities are little in evidence. But as soon as some incentive — positive or negative, encouraging or threatening — comes along, it is met by a sudden burst of energy, that may make up for everything.

4. The notorious Polish lack of common sense; a tendency to be

92

habitually guided by the impractical and illusory. But, when a Pole becomes interested in reality, or is forced to take it into account — when he has no alternative but to face it — his innate intelligence and, even more, his intuition, enable him to understand and master it with unusual skill and rapidity. Impractical though he is in everyday matters, he rises to the occasion when an unforeseen crisis occurs.

5. In every direction, then, we see spiritual richness and variety, and therefore great possibilities; but, at the same time, unpredictability, caprice, a life undisciplined by the will and some recognised standard of behaviour. It is often a matter of chance whether the good elements of the Polish character come into play or simply lie dormant.

6. But if Poles often fail to live by a deliberately chosen code of conduct, there is something in them that takes its place — a subconscious, profound, continuous emotional trend in such fundamental matters as, for instance, personal dignity or love of one's country. Instead of stability and consistency, there is an emotional inflexibility which returns doggedly — almost instinctively — to the same aims.

7. Typically Polish, too, is the romantic sense of reality — the tendency to be guided by feeling rather than by a practical outlook on the world. While this attitude may lead to disaster and disillusionment, it also enables Poles to walk unseeing over dangerous precipices, and to achieve what anyone else would think impossible.

To sum up: In the uneven Polish character, with all its amazing contrasts, there is after all a kind of precarious balance — a shifting equilibrium — caused by the fact that each group of negative elements is counteracted by positive ones, and that circumstances can sometimes change even vices to virtues.

Do we not find just these characteristics in Jim, almost as though he were a test-case?

B. The Question of Betrayal

As I have already pointed out, it is impossible to understand Conrad's problem in relation to Poland unless one has a good knowledge of Polish history and tradition, as they were conceived in Conrad's day.

In Poland (as, no doubt, in all oppressed countries) betrayal, disloyalty, desertion from the ranks, were unforgivable sins — crimes of a peculiarly grave kind.

The most dangerous threat to the life of a nation is not the declared enemy but the traitor, the renegade, the man who abandons his post. It is he who weakens, or even breaks, the inner line of defence — a line which may be political, or merely moral, but which, to a conquered country, takes the place of the armed forces and territorial frontiers on which free countries rely for their security. As we know, the first people to be "liquidated" by an underground movement — and liquidated with extreme ruthlessness — are not the invaders but the traitors and deserters.

The need for national loyalty, and the total condemnation of all who fail in it, are in direct proportion to the difficulty of enforcing it openly. In such circumstances, both the loyalty and the condemnation of disloyalty must come from the people themselves. Public opinion in a nation robbed of its statehood is a far sterner guardian of patriotic duty than the state itself could ever be.

The burning issue of national loyalty and national betrayal runs through the whole history of Poland under the yoke. The pages of this history are filled with the figures of patriots who were faithful unto death — but side by side with them we find traitors, *agents provocateurs,* and spies of every description.

The theme of treachery found its way into the works of the greatest Polish poets of the Romantic period: we need only recall Mickiewicz's *Konrad Wallenrod*, Krasiński's *Iridion* and Słowacki's *Kordian* — all of them books that Conrad must have known well in his youth. In fact, he owed his Christian name to the hero of Mickiewicz's poem. Joseph Conrad, the son of a patriot who was also a poet, must, in his childhood and early youth, have been familiar with this historical and literary tradition, which undoubtedly left a deep and lasting impression on his character and imagination.

By the time he left Poland, the young Conrad was already sensitively aware of the importance of national loyalty, and the disgrace of betrayal. Only with this in mind can we understand the significance of his own drama, and his obsessive preoccupation with the whole question, once he found himself drawn within its fatal orbit.

It is true, of course, that Conrad's fellow-countrymen could accuse him of nothing worse than abandoning his post while the country was oppressed and its people persecuted. His youthful fault could, perhaps, be best described as a failure to live up to the trust placed in him as the son of an eminent patriot; and this is very far from the ruthless verdict pronounced by Orzeszkowa.

Betrayal, in its true sense, implies going over to the enemy. England was not Poland's enemy.

But the word "betrayal" is of wide application: one can betray one's faith, one's ideals, one's flag. Conrad was not, then, beyond reproach.

The ill-omened word stuck to him, whether or not he deserved it. Whatever the objective truth of the matter, the enduring force of the accusation must be reckoned with when we consider the problem of the author of *Lord Jim*.

C. Orzeszkowa's article

To give the reader the whole picture, I should, I think, end by quoting Eliza Orzeszkowa's unfortunate article,* of which so much has been said — and without which we should not, perhaps, have *Lord Jim* in its present form.

The article was the last link in a long discussion in the press between Professor Wincenty Lutosławski and the writer Tadeusz Żuk-Skarszewski, on what was known as the "emigration of talents". Lutosławski, who had himself written, in English, a well-known work on Plato, defended the emigration of gifted Poles who left their own country for a wider field. He argued that by so doing they not only developed their own talents but won respect for Poland. As an outstanding example, he quoted the novelist Joseph Conrad Korzeniowski, whom he had visited in England.

Orzeszkowa entered the lists in 1899 with a long article in the form of an open letter published in the periodical *Kraj* (no. 16). Her thesis was that Poland, impoverished and left to her own resources, could not afford to lose her most brilliant sons to other, and more fortunate, countries. She ended by writing about Conrad:

"And, speaking of books, I must say that this gentleman, who writes, in English, novels that are widely read and that bring him in a great deal of money, has almost given me an attack of nerves. I felt, as I read about him, as though something slimy and unpleasant were creeping up my throat. What! So creative talent is to join the exodus? Up to the present we've been hearing only of engineers, lawyers and opera-singers. But it's now come to a

---

* Conrad told his niece, Aniela Zagórska, that he had also had a personal letter from Orzeszkowa; but the matter remains somewhat mysterious.

general absolution for writers. When it's a question of books on chemistry or even philosophy, I don't know much about such things, and can see that there may be something to be said for their being published in a foreign language. But when it comes to novels, containing some little spark of creative talent — well, I'm in the trade myself and know its obligations, 'forts comme la mort,' and I protest with all my heart and soul. Creative talent is the flower of the growing plant, the topmost pinnacle of the tower, the centre of the nation's heart. To take this blossom, this pinnacle, this heart, from one's own country and hand it over to the Anglo-Saxons, who have every mortal thing they want — simply because they pay more! One can't even think of it without shame. And, to make it worse, this gentleman bears the name of that very Józef Korzeniowki* over whose novels I, as a schoolgirl, shed my first tears of compassion, and felt the first ardour of generous enthusiasm and resolve. Over the novels of Mr. Conrad Korzeniowski, no Polish schoolgirl will shed altruistic tears or make noble resolutions."

The article, as we see, is narrow-minded, utterly blind to the truth about Conrad, and profoundly unjust. But it hit the mark, for this was one of those tragic conflicts in which each side is, to some extent, in the right. Many years later, when Conrad was in Zakopane, and Aniela Zagórska offered him a novel by Orzeszkowa, he burst out, "Don't give me anything by that hag! You don't know what a letter she once wrote me."

Postscript to *Lord Jim*

I cannot end my analysis of *Lord Jim* without an elucidation. This great novel undoubtedly contains my strongest argument for the hypothesis of Conrad's guilt complex in relation to his country. But it is not the only argument, nor is it indispensable. If Conrad had never written *Lord Jim* — if Orzeszkowa had never published her open letter in the press — my hypothesis would remain unaltered. As I pointed out in my discussion of *An Outcast of the Islands*, this second novel of Conrad's contained all the material I needed. For my hypothesis rested, not only on Conrad's reaction to Orzeszkowa's letter, but on the signs of conflict that one sees in his writings, from *An Outcast of the Islands* to *The Rover* — really almost all through his life.

---

* Józef Korzeniowski, a well-known novelist, unrelated to Conrad.

I repeat: whether Orzeszkowa's accusation played a major part in the writing of *Lord Jim* is a question that has no direct bearing on Ujejski's thesis, or on mine. The real question is, whether the theme of desertion and betrayal which recurs obsessively in so much of Conrad's work was, or was not, connected with the fact of his leaving Poland and devoting his talent to a foreign literature. The problem would have been almost the same if Orzeszkowa's article had never been written.

TYPHOON

Although *Typhoon* is the apparently straightforward story of the heroic Captain McWhirr, it has, on a closer look, a twofold aspect. Conrad presents his hero as an exemplary sailor and man, but he shows the dullness and lack of intelligence of this model character so consistently that it is hard not to detect a certain veiled irony in the picture. This twofold aspect of the story — of which each aspect is undoubtedly sincere — is an obvious indication of the ambivalent attitude of the author himself.

It is easy to see that *Typhoon* grew out of the same atmosphere and the same problems that preoccupied Conrad in *Lord Jim*. *Typhoon*, his next novel, was another, though very different, link in the same chain. Jim has a rich personality, full of noble impulses, but he is also undisciplined and unpredictable, and, when put to the test, he fails. Conrad contrasts him, in the same novel, with the French naval officer who, at the risk of his life, brings in the damaged ship — the *Patna* — that Jim has abandoned. McWhirr, in the full fury of the typhoon that might wreck his ship at any moment, carries out his Captain's duties intrepidly. He and the French officer are men of the same breed; McWhirr is simply a more extreme example of loyal — indeed, blind — obedience to the rules of his calling, and of concern for the honour of a seaman.

There is a passage in *Lord Jim* which might serve as a motto for *Typhoon*: "Hang ideas! They are tramps, vagabonds knocking at the back-door of your mind, each taking a little of your substance, each carrying away some crumb of that belief in a few simple notions you must cling to if you want to live decently and would like to die easy!"*

---

* *Lord Jim*, p. 43.

The character of McWhirr is the embodiment of this attitude — that of a simple man, to whom complicated ideas mean nothing, and who, for this very reason, is able to carry out with unflinching courage the work he has undertaken to do. For this alone — for the uncompromising simplicity of his understanding of duty — Conrad sets him on a pedestal.

It is worth noticing that the contrasting approaches to the theme of *Lord Jim* appear in yet another form in *Typhoon*. Jim, so hopeful and promising when all is going well, fails utterly in two crises at sea, whereas McWhirr, who in everyday life is looked upon as a dullard, passes a most exacting test with flying colours, and, in so doing, reveals many fine qualities (as, for instance, in his very human and understanding way of dealing with the question of the coolies' property) — qualities which no one would have expected to find in so ordinary a person.

McWhirr's character is generally interpreted in only one way. Most of the critics and the general readers of *Typhoon* see its hero as the apotheosis of the ordinary man. When I first read the book, I too saw him in that way. McWhirr then seemed to me simply the expression of the author's anguished longing for the untroubled conscience and serene self-confidence of men like the Captain of the *Nan-Shan* — men who, precisely because of their ordinariness and lack of imagination, never stray from the path of duty. For there can be no doubt that the factual, objective *Typhoon* has undertones that are no less personal than those in the obviously subjective *Lord Jim*.

But on my second reading of *Typhoon* — years after my first — I was struck very forcibly by another note in it. This glorification of a blind sense of duty suddenly seemed to me to have a touch of irony — albeit an irony tempered by an indulgent smile. The book is indeed a glorification of inflexible endurance — endurance that is, however, unaccompanied by the slightest trace of foresight, or even common sense. The reason for McWhirr's determination not to steer clear of the typhoon is that he does not want to add another two hundred miles to the voyage, although by the course he has chosen he is risking the almost certain loss of both ship and men. The book is full of such ambiguous situations, in which it is hard to tell which predominates — the author's admiration, or his half-amused contempt, over so primitive an ideal. Even the remark that, when all seems lost, this heroic simpleton still retains some "vague sense of the fitness of things" may be taken in two ways. Does it not also contain an ironic note, suggesting that, in an apparently hopeless situation, it is the ordinary man, without any imagination, who comes through best?

It may of course be argued that Conrad deliberately deprived his hero of everything that could have set him apart from the common run of men, making him so humdrum as to be almost stupid, in order to bring out his simple human qualities. But it is difficult not to detect in the emphasis laid by the author on McWhirr's low mental level a shade of disdain and perhaps even of dislike — an envious dislike of the lucky fellow who knows nothing of the failings and self-torture which are the lot of more complex natures.

Typhoon marks an important stage in Conrad's inner drama. The impassioned enquiry in *Lord Jim* into the question of how far a man can rely on his own conduct, is solved, in the story of Captain McWhirr, in a humble but at least positive way. Jim's aspirations, even when crowned with success, are not yet a sufficient guarantee. Conrad evidently came to the sad conclusion that the only people who can be wholly relied on are simpletons without imagination or hampering doubts. The figure of the guileless servant of duty was to reappear, in an increasingly idealised form, in many of Conrad's books, right up to its romantic apotheosis in Lingard in the final version of *The Rescue*. Nowhere, however, do we see so clearly as in *Typhoon* the ambiguity of the author's attitude to his hero — an attitude full of respect, but not without a touch of condescension. Conrad already knew that the only solution was to live one's life by a few simple ideas, but he did not yet seem able to accept unreservedly so shallow an answer, nor to stifle his involuntary contempt for the man who was the personification of this impoverished principle.

Typhoon is a tale as simple as its hero's personality. As regards its artistic achievement, one can only say that Captain McWhirr, in spite of the author's conflicting attitudes, is real in everything that he feels and does; and that the description of the storm is — as always in Conrad's books — superb.

"FALK"

I have written elsewhere of the spell exercised over Conrad's literary imagination by the mythology of antiquity and the expressive force of its superhuman characters. In describing or defining the figures in his books, he often gives them names and characteristics taken from mythology. The whole of "Falk" bears the mark of a mythological allegory: the abduction of a beautiful nymph by a wild and virile centaur. The author, indeed, often refers to Falk — the owner of a tug in an Eastern port — as Hercules, or a centaur: and the niece of Hermann — a German whose ship Falk takes out of port — reminds one, in her calm beauty, of a classical statue. And, like a statue, she never says a word. The story of the love between these two strong, simple, and beautiful people is set in an Olympian atmosphere of space and freedom which contrasts strikingly with the bourgeois vulgarity of the Hermanns' home.

But these demigods, these magnificent human bodies, live in a world alien to them, surrounded by its hypocrisy and entangled in its complicated moral laws: and therein lies the drama of the tale. On the body of a Hercules, Falk has the head of an anchorite, wasted by the curse of an inhuman act; and the Diana from the Hermanns' boat is caught up in the shallowness and hypocrisy of a middle-class family.

Again, under the cover of a serene Greek legend, we have the tragic guilt, the "misfortune" which overshadows and complicates the hero's life. The story might be given the sub-title, "The concept of guilt in the world of the primitive." "Falk" is yet another variation on the theme of *Lord Jim*. Conrad seems once more to be asking himself how consciences that are totally different from each other would react to the sense of guilt — how it would affect people of different races and callings, and living in different conditions. In "Falk" he tries to show how it would be borne, not by the sensitive, ambitious Jim, but by the primitive, uncomplicated Falk. The answer is the same — even in the world of pagan demigods, there is no escape from the anguish caused by conscience.

But another point strikes us: Can we really speak of conscience here? In "Falk" we are shown an unusual and fascinating picture of the first encounter between the world of strong, simple passions animating splendid bodies, and the sphere of moral problems, where guilt and punishment already exist. We are, so to speak, watching the dawn of morality, and observing its first glimmerings. For Falk has not as yet any real sense of guilt, or any remorse over his "sin". He thinks that in his desperate fight for life in a ship lost in mid-ocean, he had a right to do as he did — to kill and eat human flesh, in order to survive. What happened was simply a "misfortune" — a disaster which caused him to break the eternal commandment of mankind which forbids the eating of another man's body. This disaster costs him the good opinion of the world, and ruins his own life by filling him with a sense of shame that to him was incomprehensible. In Falk's primitive pagan world, one can hardly speak of moral consciousness or individual conscience: there is only submission — and by no means unresisting sub- mission — to generally accepted standards. Falk's discovery of morality comes through his sensitiveness to the opinion of other people, which has power over even such a barbarian and solitary as himself. This, Conrad seems to say, is how it all began.

The *motif* of sensitiveness to the opinion of others, and the need for their respect, trust and admiration is already familiar to us from *Lord Jim*. Even the epigraph of *Lord Jim* about the importance of other people's belief points to it. Conrad keeps returning to the subject, from *Lord Jim* to *Nostromo*; it seems to have as much fascination for him as the problem of guilt itself. Here too, as in the matter of conscience, Falk is an extreme example, and all the more convincing for being so. He despises other people and is aloof and self-reliant, but he cannot live without the respect of others, and without confiding his misery to someone; nor can he marry the girl he loves without confessing his guilt. Even Falk cannot break the bond between himself and the rest of mankind; he cannot live entirely alone. Here, of course, we are reminded of yet another problem in Conrad's books — the problem of loneliness, which is a dominant feature in all his work.

It is significant that on this occasion the author's sympathies are entirely on the side of the unwitting transgressor. Conrad writes with special bitterness of his hero's chief adversary — the uncle of the beautiful girl. In the description of Hermann's unimaginative and callous reaction to Falk's confession, we see Conrad's hatred of those whose obtuseness and smug self-satisfaction make them incapable of understanding and forgiving the tragic misdeed that has ruined the life of another man. In *Lord Jim* Conrad-Marlow tries to retain a certain objectivity in his relation to the hero, of whom he is at once the accuser and the defender. Between the lines of Falk's story, we see only the author's anger at man's pitiless morality, so quick to condemn, so often less admirable than the one condemned. We may suppose that this was a very personal reaction.

But in spite of its note of drama, the story is, on the whole, serene; it even has what is rare in Conrad — a happy ending. The beautiful bodies, eager for life, triumph over the attempts of hypocritical morality to ensnare them. (The author's delight in his subject can be felt on almost every page of "Falk".) The centaur carries off his nymph to the open sea.

A PERSONAL RECORD

Authors, like politicians, usually write their reminiscences when they are old and their creative force is on the decline. In 1908, when Conrad began to write *Some Reminiscences* (a title later changed to *A Personal Record*), he was at the height of his powers, and already engaged on one of his best novels, *Under Western Eyes*. Why did he decide, halfway through his literary career, when his achievements as a novelist were far from complete, to turn to autobiography and write his reminiscences? There must have been some very good reason for his doing so.

He was fifty at the time. He had made an assured position for himself in the world of English letters, and knew that his future lay in England. His sons were growing up and beginning to understand. The time had come for him to state his relationship with Poland clearly and unambiguously — first, in order to ensure that his children understood and respected their father's decision; then, for those close to him, whose opinion he valued; and, finally, for all his readers — not only the English ones, but perhaps, at some future time, the Polish. We should remember Conrad's favourite quotation, taken from Novalis: "It is certain my conviction gains infinitely the moment another soul will believe in it".

Although Conrad's work had touched, often and from many angles, on the subject of loyalty to one's country, the allusions, always disguised, were so indefinite that they lent themselves to a variety of interpretations and were no defence against the accusations of his contemporaries, and — possibly — of posterity.

Most people would have preferred to ignore so painful and embarrassing a subject. But not Conrad. He had long since passed through the crisis of strong feeling and defensiveness into which he had been thrown by Orzeszkowa's accusation of desertion and betrayal, and was able to look at it with mature detachment. As we see from *A Personal Record*, he had surmounted it, explained it to himself, and was now able to explain it to other people. It was at last possible for him to speak of it openly. The years 1908-9 were not like the period of *Lord Jim* — that time of anguished endeavour to establish his own truth — but were rather a period of defensive crystallisation, during which he set himself to solve an unpleasant problem. His sense of having made the right decision in choosing England was strengthened by his increasing success; the arguments in his favour were becoming more and more apparent.

Conrad in Zakopane. Drawing by K. Górski.

It was now the world's judgement of him that he wanted to challenge, rather than the reproaches of his own conscience — the reproaches that he had hitherto faced only under the incognito of a fictional character. The moment had at last come for him to give a public and authoritative version of the whole affair.

In thus defining his aim in writing *A Personal Record*, we feel that we are on the right track. The two principal themes which keep appearing in this leisurely narrative are the account of his leaving Poland, to serve, later, in the British merchant navy; and the account of his writing his first novel in English. Why, among all the innumerable events of his life, did he choose those particular subjects? The choice cannot have been accidental. In *A Personal Record* he undoubtedly wanted to explain and justify these two matters, or rather this one matter — his twofold desertion of his country.

In any attempt we may make to understand the problem, *A Personal Record* is, therefore, a document of great importance. In it, Conrad clearly — we may almost say, officially — defines his position and puts forward his main line of defence, arrived at over many years of uncertainty and mental torment.

Here, greatly simplified, are the arguments which he used.

1. He was acting in obedience to a mysterious inner voice — the voice which, like the "Daimonion" of Socrates, points out the right road in the chief crises of our lives. Thus, an inexplicable impulse led Conrad to begin his first novel, just as earlier an equally inexplicable impulse had made him leave Poland to become an English seaman.

2. He threw the whole weight of reproach and self-reproach, if any, on his youthful abandonment of his country, rather than on his choice of a language to write in. Youth is, after all, irresponsible, and all its actions are ennobled by the glow of romanticism.

The moment Conrad took up this position, he became invulnerable. The mysterious irrationality of impulse virtually absolved him from reponsibility for the actions it had inspired — actions all the easier to absolve in as much as the decisions behind them were the lightly taken, romantic decisions of youth. But the decision of his mature years — the choice of a language for his books (and he stressed, even more strongly, the irrationality of this decision, too) was kept out of his critical analysis, as though it had no possible connection with the charge of desertion.

Most of these arguments — the irrationality of impulse, the irresponsibility of youth, the affirmation of a romantic attitude to life — are familiar to us from *Lord Jim* although there they appear in different proportions and are handled with less assurance. The resemblance — one may say the identity — between the two apologies — that of the fictional Jim and that of Conrad himself — is worth noticing, if only because it demonstrates once again, and this time beyond all doubt, the closeness of the link between *Lord Jim* and the author's personal problems.

In addition to Conrad's choice of profession, and, later, of the language in which he was to write, we find, in the *Personal Record*, subsidiary themes, of which, significantly, he writes more openly and convincingly than of the main ones. He has much to say about his Polish forebears and Poland in general, and does all he can to show his English readers that the tradition, history and culture that lie behind him are not to be despised. In this account of his Polish background there is a note of deep piety towards the country and people that he had left, and to whom he owed so much: and with this piety there went a desire to show, by commemorating both country and people in his writings, that he had never forgotten them. *A Personal Record* is, then, something more than an apologia; it is the settlement of an outstanding debt. By writing it, he wiped out his accounts with the past — some by payment, others by cancellation.

A Personal Record was undoubtedly a crisis — a kind of catharsis — in the history of Conrad's complex over Poland. It publicly wound up the whole affair and gave him a sense of liberation, in so far as this was possible to a man of his sensitive conscience (he says, in the same book, "I catch myself in hours of solitude and retrospect meeting arguments and charges made thirty-five years ago by voices now for ever still; finding things to say that an assailed boy could not have found simply because of the mysteriousness of his impulses to himself").* It is, however, a fact that from that time the twin themes of betrayal and guilt appear less frequently in his work, and never with the same note of urgency, or in so obviously personal a form.

One puts the book down with mixed feelings. There can be no doubt of its astonishing courage and sincerity. Conrad did not shrink from touching on the most sensitive areas of his life. He uses bitter words — lack of patriotism, desertion, betrayal. And

---

* *A Personal Record*, p. 121.

although he deals with these subjects cautiously and in general terms, hinting at what he had in mind rather that saying it outright, one could hardly ask more of him. His aversion "to show his wounds to the crowd", as he himself described it to Arthur Mee, is quite comprehensible, compels our respect, and adds to the significance of the admissions that he forced out of himself.

There is something else that surprises the reader. These astonishingly frank confidences are lacking in the note of direct and unguarded sincerity. Their animation, pathos and irony often seem overdone — almost forced. He obviously wants, at all costs, to give the impression that he is treating his subject with the utmost freedom, but one looks in vain (except in purely descriptive or reminiscent passages) for freedom and naturalness in what purports to be spontaneous story-telling. Yet one would think that Conrad, a master — almost the inventor — of the *gavenda* novel, would express himself more easily and unconstrainedly than ever in his reminiscences — reminiscence being the most natural form of *gavenda*. But one is disappointed. *A Personal Record* may be among his most admirable books from the moral standpoint, but it is difficult not to feel the moral and artistic strain behind some of the most personal parts of it.

Let us look at the matter in detail.

The beginning of the book is flawless, casual, relaxed, natural — a true *gavenda*. The impression of insincerity starts only with Chapter IV, when Conrad, having already told us, in Chapter I, the romantic story of the manuscript of his first novel, now sets out to describe how he came to write it, and tries, by all the means in his power, to convince us that it happened on an inexplicable impulse, without any previous intention or discoverable reason.

In the preceding Chapter III (the dramatic and touching story of his family) Conrad is deeply sincere and the narrative flows easily. Even when he deals with the subject of his leaving Poland to become an English seaman, his style is assured and straightforward. It was a subject he could still face unperturbed. The trouble started at the second stage of the problem of "desertion" — the stage at which he became an English writer.

Here the tone changes. Conrad tries to treat the subject casually, in an almost jocular way, but his light-heartedness and wit sound artificial and strained and the whole story of his embarking "involuntarily" on English letters is unconvincing.

When, in the last part of Chapter IV, the Almayer episode is introduced, Conrad immediately regains his ease and fluency of expression. The account of his meeting with Almayer is a little masterpiece.

At the beginning of Chapter V Conrad returns to the dominant theme of the book — the genesis of *Almayer's Folly:* and the forced and obviously artificial jocularity of tone returns, too. And, once indulged, this unmistakable insincerity continues even when Conrad enters on a subject as serious and important to a writer as his artistic and philosophical credo. Thus, instead of being the best, Chapters IV and V are on the whole the least convincing in the book.

After one's first surprised reaction one sees why it is so. To Conrad, with his proud and deeply reserved nature, the writing of this kind of apologia for his abandonment of his native literature was an effort rather than a joy, and the weakness of the relevant parts of the book shows exactly where the point of painful tension lay. One might almost say that Conrad wrote these pages with his lips compressed and his imagination shackled. As we may remember, he himself said, in *A Familiar Preface* to *Some Reminiscences*, that there are writers "to whom an open display of sentiment is repugnant"*)**

How great, then, must have been his need to settle, through this book, his acount with Poland, if, in spite of this inner resistance, he completed his task!

A Personal Record must, of course, be read almost like a palimpsest. Its importance and revealing quality lie not only in what it says with so much effort. Equally important and revealing is what underlies the text — what could not be said outright — what the author may not even have allowed himself to think.

Perhaps the most striking instance of this is the fact that I have already mentioned, that the only accusation that Conrad speaks of in *A Personal Record* is the charge of his having gone off to sea. The whole question of his possible "guilt" was confined to that — although, as Ujejski first pointed out, he might have spent his whole life sailing under a foreign flag without thereby showing the least disloyalty to his own country. If disloyalty came into the matter at all, it lay in his handing over his creative talent — his soul, as it were — to a foreign literature.

---

* *A Personal Record*, p. XVI.
** There is, significantly, a similar note of restraint alternating with sudden outbursts of emotion in the only story which Conrad wrote about Poland and a Polish hero: "Prince Roman" (1910).

Perhaps, if we are to understand the alternation throughout *A Personal Record* of heroic frankness and flight into the uncharted territory of irrational impulse, we must fall back on half-conscious, or even unconscious, processes. The evasive action taken by the mind is best seen from without; from within, it usually encounters blind spots in the vision. Except in the case of cynics, this is so with everybody — even with people whose consciences are unusually sensitive. Without some such inner defence mechanism it would be hard to live at all — and hardest for those who are the most uncompromising, the most severe towards themselves.

A CHANGE IN CONRAD'S ATTITUDE
TO THE SUBJECT OF BETRAYAL

At the time when he was writing *A Personal Record*, Conrad returned, in *Under Western Eyes*, to the obsessive theme of loyalty and betrayal. But here he wrote of it in a completely different frame of mind. The problem of betrayal, although presented more sharply and unequivocally than in any of his other books, does not seem to involve him very closely. It is seen from the outside, from the point of view of a spectator, instead of being anxiously debated within his own conscience.

Of the novel itself, I shall write elsewhere. What at present concerns me is the author's complete change of attitude in relation to his subject. From the first pages of the book, it is quite obvious that Conrad felt closer to, more inwardly at one with, the suffering of the uncivilized Karain or the primitive Falk than with the fears of the student Razumov, whom, apart from an occasional flicker of sympathy, he regards with cold, inexorable detachment — even, at times, with aversion — until love and suffering have transformed him.

It is true that this emotional remoteness, this non-involvement of the author in the drama of guilt and betrayal, may, to some extent, have been caused by the moral and racial "otherness" of Razumov (we must not forget Conrad's intense dislike, not only of Russia as a state, but of her whole moral atmosphere). On the other hand, to ascribe what had been so deeply personal, a preoccupation of so many years standing, to someone as alien to himself as Razumov, is a sign that the preoccupation itself had become more objective and had ceased to torment him.

Under Western Eyes has an interesting parallel in *An Outcast of the Islands*, a story Conrad had written almost fifteen years before. In both works his attitude to the problem of betrayal, and to the man guilty of betrayal is equally detached and critical.

When Conrad wrote *An Outcast,* the sense of tragic guilt had not yet fully emerged from his subconscious, nor, until Orzesz-kowa's article, was it sufficently embittered to draw him into the orbit of the fictional hero of the drama. I have discussed the matter at greater length in an earlier chapter.

When working on *Under Western Eyes* in the liberating atmosphere of *A Personal Record,* Conrad had settled his accounts with Poland, and, to a great extent, overcome his feeling of guilt, so that he was again able to write about the subject from an impersonal distance.

The two works, written with fifteen years between them, form a kind of prologue and epilogue to what I have called the theme of *"Lord Jim"*. It is worth noting that they also mark the beginning and end of the period in which Conrad wrote his best books. To the biographer, the chief value of these two severe and condemnatory versions of a drama of betrayal lies in the fact that they show so clearly the uncompromising moral background against which Conrad's own drama was enacted, and that they make it possible for us to sound its full depth.

VICTORY

1.

By a strange meeting of opposites, the problem of Shakespeare's *Hamlet* came very close to the fearless man who, in early youth, after standing up to the united disapproval of his family, left his own country to travel all over the world and to contend for years, first with the perils of the sea, and then with the indifference of the public, until he came out victorious. Let us look at both sides of the problem.

Yet throughout Conrad's works there appears the theme familiar to us from *Hamlet* — the dread of taking action, the inability to seize the right moment for making decisions, and the paralysing power of thought and imagination over the will. From *Almayer's Folly* and *Lord Jim* up to *Victory* and the *Shadow Line*, Conrad's books are full of situations that might have come straight out of *Hamlet*. The central figure, when in some grave danger, always delays and deliberates endlessly, instead of acting. The constant recurrence of this theme, which is examined from every angle and embodied in a succession of characters, makes one suspect Conrad's personal involvement.

On the other hand, it is also true that his books contain such characters as McWhirr and Lingard, men who are inflexibly loyal to duty, and on whom Conrad's popularity as a writer chiefly rests. But many of the characters created by the author of *Victory* are weak, temporizing and harassed by doubts and fears — people to whom heroism and intransigent morality represent an agonisingly unattainable ideal.

Although these matters are too well-known to need more than a brief mention, they form a starting-point. One further point is perhaps worth recalling — Conrad's devotion to Shakespeare. A volume of his complete works was one of the few books that accompanied Conrad on all his voyages; from Shakespeare he learnt his English; and if any English writer influenced the language and imagination of the great intruder into English literature, it was certainly Shakespeare.

We can easily guess which Shakespearian play affected young Conrad most profoundly. Let us think for a moment what the reading of *Hamlet* must have meant to the son of parents persecuted by Russia, and what reflections on his own life and character must have been aroused by this drama of neglected vengeance. Every scene in the strangely similar story must have entered deep into his soul.

Nevertheless, it is to Conrad's own personality, rather than to the tragedy in his family, that we should trace the Hamlet-like quality of so many of his characters.

Hamlet owes his innumerable descendants in the world of literature to the fact that almost everyone who is an artist by nature is called on to experience something of his drama. The meaning of *Hamlet* is, of course, open to endless interpretations. The interpretation which, to me, seems to come closest to Shakespeare's own conception is that which sees the unhappy Dane as a typical poet and thinker — a man of imagination, feeling, and an enquiring mind — who suddenly finds himself faced with the terrible duty of taking action ("O cursed spite, that ever I was born to set it right"). His vocation is to see and analyse — at most, to stage a drama that will prick the conscience of the royal murderer. But hardly to act!

Shakespeare perhaps put more of himself into *Hamlet* — the poet at odds with life — than into any other of his plays. This seems to me the main reason for the influence that the play had on Conrad. Influences in literature — creative literature — are, above all, a matter of psychological kinship. Conrad, the son of a poet, and himself a born artist — exposed, like all artists, to "the slings and arrows of outrageous fortune" — found his own personality portrayed in Shakespeare's tragedy.

Let us remember, too, that Conrad's life was not an easy one. He had, throughout his youth and early manhood, to meet the exacting demands and to bear the responsibilities of a sailor's vocation, and, later, those of a writer working in the unfamiliar, and therefore difficult, conditions of a foreign country. At first, no doubt, while the energy and romantic enthusiasm of youth — as yet unaware of its artistic vocation — stifled the dichotomy between thought and action, it was possible for him to ignore the conflict. But later — particularly after he had passed the "shadow line"? For one burdened with Conrad's sweeping imagination — that "mother of fears" and of the destructive power of thought — it must have been hard to struggle on, day after day, with the petty toils and worries of life.

Nor was this all. The resemblances to Hamlet of the man who wrote *Victory* were quite exceptional. His whole life had been overshadowed by the tragedy of his childhood, and was further darkened by the accusation of abandoning his oppressed country and leaving his parents' deaths unavenged. His youthful self-confidence had been shaken almost as soon as he left Poland, by his failure in Marseilles, which shattered his ambitions and cost him his uncle's confidence.

Another man would soon have forgotten these youthful follies — but not Conrad. His uncle, Tadeusz Bobrowski, had often warned him of the tendency to melancholy and pessimism that he had inherited from his father. His uncle's letters, as well as Conrad's own, and the account given us by his wife, suggest that another element may have strengthened this tendency — the cyclic disposition so often found in artists, whose periods of intense creative activity are often followed by a reaction of profound depression. In such dark moments, every action, every decision, becomes an almost intolerable burden, leading to situations that might have come straight out of *Hamlet*. Conrad's son John told me that on one of those bad days his father had to go to the dentist with toothache. He walked up and down in front of the surgery for an hour, unable to make up his mind to go in. At last he dropped the idea, and went home.

Even the "irrational impulses" to which Conrad attributed such importance in his life, and which seemed to be due to superabundant vitality, may, in many cases, have been crises caused by the anguish of prolonged indecision — the snapping of an over-strained cord.

Do we not see similar — and, to all appearances, equally inexplicable — reactions in Hamlet — the sudden stabbing of Polonius, the adventure on the ship, the duel with Laertes?

The list of analogies is long, and surely needs no further additions. But its limits need to be defined. Any attempt to find a single pattern for Conrad's psychology will end by misleading us. The familiar figure of an intrepid sailor, taking dangerous decisions lightheartedly — almost rashly — seems utterly unlike the man whom I have tried to discuss here. Conrad's exemplary behaviour in the merchant navy has never been questioned. Even in his later, more settled life, he was impulsive, pugnacious, and fearlessly brave — quite prepared to fight a duel with Wells over a mere trifle, or to go off during the war, regardless of his age and broken health, in pursuit of German submarines.

All these incongruous and discordant elements were contained in his complex nature. One almost feels that as many different characters could have been extracted from his single personality as swarm through his books. But it is also certain that we should never have had Almayer, Jim, Decoud or Heyst if Conrad had not carried them all within himself, and known, to its depth, the torture of indecision, nervous collapse and disbelief in everything. One side of him — the sailor's *sans peur et sans reproche* — was shown to the world; the other side remained in the background, almost wholly hidden, and discernible mainly in his work.

2.

The subject of this chapter is *Victory*, the last of several of Conrad's works whose theme links them with *Lord Jim*. In this second section, I want to discuss those elements which abound in *Victory* as nowhere else in Conrad, and which he took from his own life or personality. I will begin, however, by summarising the plot, for this will help us later to trace the analogies between the book and its author.

Axel Heyst, the hero, taught by his philosopher father to distrust life, spends his own as a detached observer. But his detachment is broken into by compassion (against which his father had warned him) for an unsophisticated girl called Lena, who plays in an orchestra, and whom he meets by chance during one of his brief excursions to the mainland from the lonely island on which he lives. To save the girl from the brutal leader of the orchestra and the amorous importunities of the hotel manager, Schomberg, Heyst takes her back with him to the island — followed, however, by a gang of ruffians sent after them by the vindictive Schomberg, to rob Heyst of the fortune that he is thought to possess. The exponent of the uncommitted life does not want to — indeed, cannot — defend himself, although he is greatly concerned to save Lena. His own life he does not care about, but he feels responsible for her; and she has fallen in love with him.

There is not much that he can do (he is not even armed), but when, once or twice, there is a chance for him to act, he throws it away in a fit of apathy or scruples. His distrust of life, and his refusal to become involved, have sapped his will and made him unable to defend himself. Indeed, they have done more — they have almost robbed him of the capacity to feel deeply. For although Heyst acted out of genuine compassion and in fact has begun to live with Lena, he is unable really to love her. It is Lena herself who solves the apparently hopeless situation by saving him at the cost of her life — an action followed by a chain of consequences which ends in the destruction of the evil gang. Heyst, filled with grief and a sense of guilt, throws himself into the flames of the burning house in which Lena died.

Such is the plot of Conrad's novel, of which even the ending — a scene strewn with corpses — reminds us of Shakespeare's *Hamlet*.

In *Victory*, the Hamlet motif, which occurs in so many of Conrad's writings, is worked out more deliberately than in any other, although in a way that is at some variance with Shakespeare's own conception. The reason for this lies in the different approaches that the two writers take to the subject. Shakespeare's Hamlet is simply the portrait of a character, either observed or imaginary, that he did not try to interpret; Conrad's conception of Heyst is more consciously realised, and we are given clear indications of the influences that have made his mind and conduct what they are.

We see, from the first chapters, that Heyst's disinclination for action — and, later, his inability to take action — are due, not to his innate disposition, but to an intellectual principle. His downfall is the inevitable consequence of a planned and lengthy rejection of action, which in time has led, as surely as physical inactivity leads to muscular atrophy, to a Hamlet-like weakening of the will.

But this difference between the principles underlying Conrad's novel and Shakespeare's play does not alter the fact that the reactions of the two heroes to the test of action are fundamentally the same. The analogies between the two works are many and obvious; certain sayings — even certain scenes — are strikingly similar. We may recall just one, in which Heyst, afraid of being accused of murdering innocent men, forbears to ambush and attack the members of the gang. We are irresistibly reminded of Hamlet's scruple against killing his uncle as he kneels at prayer, for to kill him at such a time would be to send him straight to heaven.

But, as I have pointed out, the Hamlet element is not the only personal theme in *Victory*. Even for a book by Conrad, it contains an astonishing number of personal details. In the character of Heyst himself, there are many resemblances to the author, besides the Hamlet-like quality. Stefan Kołaczkowski, one of the most perceptive critics in pre-war Poland, wrote, as far back as 1925: "Even if not a single scene in Heyst's life bore the slightest resemblance to any situation in the life of the author, Heyst would still remain the most subjective expression of Conrad's spirit and general attitude, and of the truth concerning the contradictions in his nature, although perhaps in a deliberately different relationship".

This fits in. We shall not be far out if we say that Conrad left us two self-portraits — one, in *Lord Jim,* as a young man, and the other, of his maturity, in *Victory*.

Let us try to see, roughly, how much of Conrad there is in Heyst. I cannot begin better than by again quoting Kołaczkowski. "Heyst's apparently cold, stoical, disdainful attitude to the world hides the same capacity for intense feeling for mankind — the same shy reverence for all that is deeply human — that we feel in Conrad".

There is more to it than this.

"Look on — make no sound," the elder Heyst had told his son. "This world for the wise is nothing but an amusing spectacle".* "An intelligent observer of the facts" — such was the programme that Heyst set for himself. Readers of Conrad have met with this idea elsewhere. In his *Personal Record* he sees the world simply as a spectacle — the only alternative to the ethical view of the universe, which, he says, involves us in so many contradictions as to be untenable. And this innate and deeply personal point of view, which saw life as a panorama of changing scenes, Conrad transferred to his hero.

Heyst was a recluse. Not only did he escape to a lonely island, but he went through life distrustfully, cherishing his isolation. In the case of Conrad, solitude in the midst of people was the dominant theme of his life and art. Yet both Conrad and his hero were unable to pass through the suffering and injustice of this world without becoming involved.

---

* *Victory*, p. 199.

Within these broad outlines, which suggest the whole drama of Heyst — the supposed misanthrope, who is undone by pity — we find many other psychological characteristics of the hero of *Victory* to interest those in search of analogies between Conrad and his fictional double.

Heyst the romantic, who cares more for dignity than for life, and is at once courteous and aloof, was closely modelled on the author. All who knew Conrad agree that he was exactly like that, with the courtesy and dignity of an earlier day, but with a way of suddenly retreating within himself and becoming distant and inaccessible. "Conrad the romantic" are words too often used of him to need any explanation. "Dignity" is a word continually on Heyst's lips, and dignity is the mainspring of his conduct. We see it, in different forms, as the chief problem in many of Conrad's books: as pride in *Lord Jim*; as vanity in *Nostromo*; as honour in "The Duel" and *Chance*; as ambition in Razumov in *Under Western Eyes*; or simply as a need for the respect and recognition of other people (an almost invariable theme in Conrad's writing). Only a problem that touched the author very closely could recur with such insistence.

Heyst is peculiarly sensitive to any breath of slander. When Lena tells him of the rumour, passed on to her by Schomberg, of his having murdered Morrison, Heyst cannot get over it, ludicrous though it is; he returns obsessively to the subject, and at last bursts out almost hysterically to the leader of the gang of bandits: "This diabolical calumny will end in actually and literally taking my life from me."[*] We are reminded of Orzeszkowa's accusation, which weighed so heavily on Conrad.

Heyst admits, on one occasion, that there is a strain of freakishness in his character. The impulsive help that he gives, first to Morrison and then to Lena, in spite of his principle of never becoming involved in other people's affairs, certainly has this mark. In Conrad, as he himself said, such unpredictability was part of his character and fate; the most important decisions of his life were made at the prompting of irrational impulses.

One could go on finding analogies between Heyst and Conrad, but what I have said is surely enough. The resemblances, amounting at times almost to identity, are incontestable, and have long been noted by students of Conrad.

The analogies between the author and his work do not end here. Not only elements of character but details taken from Conrad's life

---

[*] *Victory*, p. 429.

Conrad in 1913, when he was working on Victory.

are to be found in *Victory* in far greater numbers than in any other of his writings, with the exception of those which, like "Youth" or *The Shadow Line*, are clearly autobiographical.

The most striking instance of this fact is the inclusion in *Victory*, with the minimum of alteration, of memories as intimate and painful as those of Conrad's last years with his father. Almost everything that Conrad tells us about the elder Heyst (an element of the novel which plays a very important part in the book, for the younger Heyst's whole life is affected by his father's attitude) is taken from Conrad's own experience — even to the burning of his father's papers.

Where the past is concerned, then, Conrad identifies himself with his hero almost completely, and without disguise. In defining his present position, the author is more discreet, for reasons not difficult to guess.

Here he adopts the same symbolic pattern that he has already used in *Lord Jim* (the return to this pattern is in itself significant) — the island, the peaceful atmosphere at last restored, the invasion of rapacious and ruthless elements from the world that he has left, and, finally, the loving and courageous woman, who wants to defend and save the indecisive man, restrained as he is by motives past her comprehension. One is reminded, almost involuntarily, of England, where the author has made a home and won fame; the intruders from the outer world (perhaps even his own importunate fellow-countrymen) accusing him of desertion and the betrayal of his country, and, last but not least, Jessie, who must often have said to her over-scrupulous husband, with his conscience at war with itself, "Forget the past. Hold on to your happiness, and if anyone tries to trouble it, take no notice; don't give in — fight!"

The above are some outstanding examples of the way in which Conrad made use of situations and incidents from his own life, as unreservedly as he transplanted elements of his personality into that of his hero. This list, as it stands, is long enough to show that *Victory* reveals more of Conrad than any other of his books. This is an important discovery and will help us in the further analysis of the novel.

3.

I am now coming to the central problem of the book and the core of my study. What is the true meaning of *Victory*, and what was its origin? If an author writes what is more or less his self-portrait in fiction and then draws some moral lesson from it, we are entitled to think that here, too, he has himself in mind.

Everything that I have so far said has been leading up to this conclusion. Conrad never merely reproduces reality, nor is he a lover of psychological analysis for its own sake. He is a poet of the drama and meaning of life. Apart from the dramatic effect itself, what is the meaning that he wants to express in *Victory?*

It seems quite unambiguous. He himself proclaims it with a directness and clarity rare in his books: "Woe to the man whose heart has not learned while young to hope, to love — and to put its trust in life!"*

The obvious lesson to be learnt from Heyst's story is, then, one of total rejection of an attitude of indifference to life. Anyone who tries to retreat from life to the position of a passive spectator must, sooner or later, pay the price of his withdrawal, for life always takes its revenge on those who, by avoiding its challenge, have left themselves weak and unprepared — just as those who have coddled instead of hardening themselves are the first to be attacked by frost. Moreover, a refusal to face life entails not only external but emotional loss; it not only causes the will to degenerate but destroys the ability to feel profoundly. Such, in brief, is the moral thesis of *Victory*.

The title, closely linked with the meaning of the book, is equally unambiguous. The word appears several times in the text — always in scenes of decisive importance, and always in connection with Lena. Lena conquers by her love, by her profound emotional involvement — the most powerful motive force in human action. Heyst's incapacity for action is due, at least in part, to the inadequacy of his emotional response — his inability to love deeply. His defeat is the defeat of indifference.

Attempts have, indeed, been made to give an ironic twist to the title *Victory*. There is nothing in the book to support such an interpretation. It is true that in Conrad's complex view of life we can see the doubt behind every affirmation. But the question that concerns us is what meaning he himself intended to convey by the theme and title of the book — and this meaning is unmistakable; Lena's moral triumph is contrasted with Heyst's defeat in such a way as to rule out all possibility of misunderstanding.

Moreover, in the author's note to *Victory* in the collected edition of his works published in 1920, he again leaves the point beyond all doubt: "Heyst in his fine detachment had lost the habit

---

* *Victory*, p. 460.

122

of asserting himself . . . the readiness of the mind and the turn of the hand that come without reflection and lead the man to excellence in life . . . Thinking is the great enemy of perfection. The habit of profound reflection, I am compelled to say, is the most pernicious of all the habits formed by the civilised man."*

"Woe to the man whose heart has not learned . . . to put its trust in life," says Heyst, just before he commits suicide. If we agree that Heyst is Conrad's mouthpiece, this is indeed an astonishing statement. All Conrad's books, up to that time, had shown the author's deep distrust of life, which to him was like the sea itself — lulling a man one day, and drowning him the next. It is true that Conrad made the characters in his books fight to the end against the treachery of fate — whatever happened, they had to go on steering the ship; but this was simply in the name of human dignity, not out of any naive belief that they could, in any sense whatever, emerge victorious from the unequal contest. When, as in "Falk" and *Chance*, fate spared his heroes, it did so by a rare and happy accident — by chance, in fact. But as for trusting the sea — or trusting life? The idea seems to contradict all that we know of the author's attitude, which became, perhaps, more resigned and indifferent as time went on — but certainly not more trustful.

How, then, are we to understand this sudden, diametrical change? There must surely have been some upheaval in Conrad's inner life to account for such a thing.

Let us look first at some of the biographical data. In March 1912, Conrad finished *Chance*, which in January of the same year began to come out in instalments in the *New York Herald*. It was the first of his books to become widely popular and to be a financial success. A few weeks later — in May — he started on *Victory*. This, like *Lord Jim*, he originally intended to be quite short, but it gathered momentum as he wrote it, and most probably became far fuller and more profound. Still in 1912, Conrad made friends with J. H. Retinger, a Polish politician and writer, and an ardent patriot — a fact which may have rekindled Conrad's own patriotic feelings. *Victory* was finished in the last days of May 1914, just before war broke out. It so happened that, just at that time, Retinger invited Conrad to stay with him in Cracow, and Conrad decided to take all his family with him to Poland. He left England on the eve of the outbreak of war, which caught him in Cracow.

* *Victory*, p. X.

Relating these events to his inner life, we can assume that, before starting on *Victory*, and in the early stages of writing it, Conrad must have gone through the most peaceful period of his troubled life. By writing his *Personal Record* he had ended the inner conflict that had tortured him for years, and introduced some kind of order into his harrowing and involved relationship with Poland. In two novels of the same period — *The Secret Agent* and, still more, *Under Western Eyes* — he had tackled the subject — Russia — that had so blighted his childhood. And now, at last, fate was beginning to treat him more kindly. The success of *Chance* — the first of his novels to appeal to a wider public — gave him at least some financial stability, which enabled him to provide for his family. He could at last breathe freely, both materially and psychologically.

One other event in Conrad's life may have had something to do with making this period calmer and less tense. This was, indirectly, the serious nervous breakdown which in 1910 followed the two years of appalling strain that he had undergone while writing *Under Western Eyes*.

The breakdown was accompanied by an illness which, according to Jessie, nearly killed Conrad. This crisis, which lasted for several months, may well have left him with a longing for peace at any price, and a dread of any further upheaval. He himself wrote to Hugh Clifford, just after his breakdown, to say how ill he had been, and that he was beginning to see that the terrible nervous tension of the last two years had been bound to end in some such way. The relief from financial anxiety that accompanied the success of *Chance* added to the calm that followed this terrifying experience.

The calm was, of course, only relative; it was not entirely free from the storms and stresses that were a constant feature of Conrad's nature and destiny. Moreover, in these "successful" years, his health continued to give him trouble. But it is still true to say that he had entered upon an almost Olympian — or, as he perhaps saw it, bourgeois — period of his life.

In none of his previous books do we find so much easy irony as in *Chance* — the irony by which a man laughs off the absurdities of life, when he has come to see them as an unavoidable evil, and ceased to be upset by them. We sometimes catch an echo of this half-cynical irony in *Victory* — especially in the early chapters. The character of "Heyst the gentleman", whose unvarying courtesy is a polite way of cutting himself off from other people, seems exactly to correspond to Conrad's attitude at that time. We are surely justified in thinking that the Hamlet-like tendencies that were a constant feature of Conrad's inner life had by then hardened into a decision to retreat to the position of a detached observer and deliberately adopt the passivity that he ascribes to Heyst.

But *Victory* as a whole already belongs, in mood and significance, to another period. It shows that the state of relative peace did not last very long. People used to living in storm and uproar wake up alarmed in a sudden moment of silence. In much the same way, Conrad may have felt ill at ease in his Olympian calm. He, whose life had been an unceasing struggle — a battle of conflicting loyalties — most probably became perturbed by the lull between the storms — the more so, as it was the storms that kept his creative powers alive.

Anyone who has come to know Conrad as a man of exceptionally sensitive conscience will realise that sooner or later the moment had to come when his acute awareness began to sound the alarm and make him ask himself whether it was permissible or even safe to stand aside and merely look at life and describe it.

Such, in all probability, was the psychological background of *Victory*. The book is a passionate indictment of an aloof attitude to life — a novel whose theme is the revenge that life takes on those who seek peace at any price. Unless we accept some such radical change in Conrad's attitude, it will be difficult for us to imagine how — especially during that period of psychological "siesta" — he hit on the idea of a book so deeply personal and so remote in its mood from that recuperative calm. (And we must remember that it was written just after *Chance*, in which Conrad's emotional distance from his subject was so striking). Fictional themes, especially those that deal with such weighty matters, do not come from nowhere, as a mere freak of the imagination. Least of all do they do so in the case of a writer like Conrad.

If we agree that such was indeed the idea behind *Victory* in the inner life of its author, we are at once faced with another problem. In this process of inner awakening, what part, if any, was played by the question of Conrad's failure in loyalty to his country — the old accusation brought against him by Orzeszkowa and which, for so many years, was the very centre of the drama of his life?

A man aroused from sleep will often return automatically to the train of thought that was in his mind when he dozed off. As Conrad's resolution of this painful conflict had later become one of the chief factors in his psychological restoration, we may assume that the matter must have again come to the surface and played an important, if not a decisive, part in the psychological crisis through which he was then going. The matter, silenced though it had once been by the writing of *A Personal Record*, was now clamouring for re-examination and a new approach. Unless I have been wrong from beginning to end in everything I have written, this issue too, which was of such burning importance to Conrad, had to be looked at afresh.

He, who had once written to Cunninghame Graham that "the only thing open to him was to remain faithful to a lost and hopeless cause,"* may now have asked himself whether, after all, something else was permissible — that he was free to forget, to withdraw into a soothing peace, to shut Poland completely out of his life. Had the debt really been paid in full?

It is striking how repeatedly and emphatically, with an emphasis that goes far beyond the importance of this characteristic, Conrad speaks of Heyst's aloofness and emotional coldness — his growing inability to love deeply. Did Conrad apply this to himself, with some reference, at least, to the distant country whose image must have become dimmed in his memory and feelings — especially at a time when his life in England was taking a more successful turn? It may be significant, as an indication of the extent to which Poland was in his mind while he was writing *Victory*, that in none of his other books are there such clear echoes of Polish literature.**

We cannot know the exact course of this inward drama, nor can we know its outcome. There are, however, a good many significant indications in his subsequent life. His attitude to the Polish cause undoubtedly became more clearly defined, active and courageous than it had ever been before. Above all, he at last made up his mind to look Poland in the face, and show his wife and sons something of his Polish past. Almost as soon as he finished *Victory* he took them with him to Poland, where he had not been throughout the twenty

---

* G. J. Aubry, *Joseph Conrad, Life and Letters*, London, 1927. Vol. I, p. 269. "Je trouve que rien ne m'est permis hormis la fidélité à une cause absolument perdue" (Letter of 8th February 1899).
** See Andrzej Busza, *Conrad's Polish Literary Background and Some Illustrations of the Influence of Polish Literature on His Work;* (Chapter on *"Victory"*), Polish Historical Institute, Rome, 1966.

years of his married life. Retinger's invitation and Conrad's improved financial position of course counted for something, but the decision meant too much to him to be explicable by such circumstances alone.

Moreover, as I have said, Conrad's whole attitude to Polish affairs suddenly became far more definite and deeply involved. During his visit to Poland he gave a lawyer in Cracow, T. Kosch, the memorandum of a scheme he had drawn up for solving the Polish question as he saw it in the political context of the time; and he promised Kosch to arouse English public opinion in the matter. During the next few years he wrote and published several articles on the Polish question, and on his stay in Poland. Here, too, there may, of course, have been accessory motives and explanations. His feeling for Poland had been strengthened by his visit, and the war between Russia and Germany had obviously re-kindled his hopes for Poland's future. But this does not explain everything. We must look deeper. He had closed his account with Poland by writing *A Personal Record*, but he now reopened that account in an entirely different mood — a mood of hopefulness and active involvement, instead of one that was merely guilt-ridden and defensive.

The idea outlined above is, of course, hypothetical. It rests, however, on a basis of probability that should be convincing enough to secure it against immediate rejection.

This enquiry was not undertaken with a view to forming a literary judgement. *Victory*, seen purely as literature, is not one of the most successful of Conrad's works. As an idea, an intellectual conception, it certainly ranks high, but in execution and artistry it shows a falling-off of creative freedom and power; one even feels in it a certain effort, which conveys an impression of artificiality. Conrad was ageing, both as a man and as a creative writer; he was probably no longer up to handling so weighty a subject. But whatever the reasons for the weaknesses of *Victory* as a work of art, the problems it raises are of intense interest for the biographer of Conrad's inner life; and the conclusions, hypothetical though they are, that we arrive at after analysing these problems may throw a light not only on the author but on the book.

Seen from this standpoint, *Victory* holds an important place in Conrad's writings — the more so as it is the last of the searching and exhaustive arguments that he held with himself.

4.

I must, in conclusion, return to the point from which I started — the element of Hamlet in Conrad. It would be misleading and unjust to leave the matter without further comment.

In the preceding sections of this study I have tried — I hope successfully — to show Conrad's reaction to the threat of a psychological lull. It was a reaction typical of him. He no sooner saw the danger than he stood up to it. He knew all the downfalls, reverses and fears of a man's inner life, but he never gave in to any for long. He fought each in turn, and, even after a crushing defeat, went back to the attack more defiantly than ever. Such was undoubtedly his reaction to the Hamlet element he saw in himself. It was his constant companion, but he gave it no quarter. One may even say paradoxically that it was the source of his strength.

The strength was, however, dearly bought; life took its highest toll of him. It was one unending round of self-conquests, self-testings and attempts to prove, to himself and to others, his true value in the face of an ever-present doubt that he never fully overcame.

So he appears to us — the Conrad who is almost unknown. Perhaps, in spite of the self-revelations in his letters, we should never have seen him at such depth if he had not abandoned his disguise in the books that were also written in unceasing doubt and despair. Nothing came to him easily — neither life nor art. But in spite of this — or perhaps because of it — he achieved almost everything that a man can achieve, both in art and life. Doubt acted on him as a spur, urging him on to even more daring and higher achievements. And so he could change the spectre of defeat, described in so many of his books, into triumph. Of no one, perhaps, can we say more truly what he himself said of Lord Jim: he mastered his fate.

THE ROVER

The Rover, the last of Conrad's completed major works, was written, in a sudden burst of inspiration, in seven months, while he was working on a novel of the Napoleonic period.

The theme of the story is the return to post-revolutionary France of an old privateer who has spent his life on the high seas, and who now wants to end his days peacefully in the land of his birth. He is, however, caught up in the war then being waged between France and England, and the old seaman ends by laying down his life for the country which in his youth, he had abandoned.

The reader cannot fail to be struck by the similarity of the situation described in the book to that of its author (we know, from the memoirs of Conrad's wife, that he wanted, towards the end of his life, to return to Poland). *The Rover* is Conrad's swan-song. Although the critics differ widely over the place due to it in his work, no one can deny that it is a remarkable achievement, written though it was when his creative power was beginning to fail, and while he was trying unsuccessfully to finish his Napoleonic novel, *Suspense*. The achievement is partly due to the fact that *The Rover* is simpler and less ambitious than his other books. It has neither the complicated problems of *Lord Jim* nor the wide range of *Nostromo*. In *The Rover*, Conrad was content to describe the visible interplay of life, without making any great effort to look deeper under its surface.

Moreover, he set himself to write what was almost a conversation-piece — a story with few characters, in a confined space, and over a very short period of time. But it was precisely by ridding himself of the superfluities that he was able to bring the clarity and expressiveness of the action almost to the point of perfection. The beginning and end of the novel, in particular, show us Conrad at his best.

These were, however, mere technical simplifications. Those who have some knowledge of the mechanism of creative writing will have no doubt that Conrad owed this upsurge of creative power and artistic skill to the emotional background of this last novel.

It is unusually serene in tone. Even the hero's death is not presented as the tragic ending of a life, but — to quote the Spenserian epigraph of the book — as "sleep after toil": and the toil was not in vain. Such an ending is rare in Conrad. What lies behind it?

We need not look far for an explanation if we remember two historic dates — 1918, the re-birth of Poland, and 1920, her victory over Communist Russia, which secured her frontiers from the East. *The Rover* was written between 1920 and 1921.

Bearing this historical background in mind, we can see in *The Rover* both the last link in "the theme of *Lord Jim*" (so often mentioned in this book) and its happy ending.

Poland was now free, and received her prodigal son with open arms. Not only had she no reproaches for him: she gloried in his international fame. A complete edition of his works in a Polish translation was already being prepared, and the greatest living writer in Poland, Stefan Żeromski, was to write the introduction.

The debit account dating from the days of Poland's bondage was now closed for ever. It was no longer possible to link the emigration of individuals with the misfortunes of their country.

What anyone had done, or failed to do, while Poland was partitioned, now made no difference; it had not barred the road to freedom. The culprits, real or supposed, felt as if a great weight had fallen from them.

Old Peyrol returns, then, without any moral stigma attached to him, freed from all scruples and restraints, to live quietly in his own country. He has lived a full and interesting life, and has no regrets. And, when the time comes, he gives his life for his country — gives it out of belated love, freely and with pride — not as a pilgrim to Canossa atoning for a sin. In this dream of voluntary sacrifice there is a serenity and quiet happiness almost unknown to the stormy and embittered years of Conrad's early life. The catharsis — the cleansing — had been achieved. Lord Jim had found eternal rest.

ROMANCE

"This is not a boy's story"
(Conrad in a letter to Pinker).

Hundreds of articles and scores of books have been written about Conrad's works. They have been analysed, evaluated and arranged in order of their supposed merit.

Yet the great world that he created still holds surprises for us. Some of his books, hitherto regarded as unimportant, or quite simply forgotten, show, at a closer look, unsuspected depth and beauty.

Two of his novels in particular seem to me to call for re-appraisal. One is *An Outcast of the Islands*; the other, *Romance*. Here I propose to examine *Romance* a little more closely.

The general opinion is that, written as it was in collaboration with Ford Madox Ford and being therefore only in part Conrad's work, it is not worthy of serious attention. Jocelyn Baines, the author of the excellent book on Conrad to which I have referred several times, says of it: "There is something unsatisfactory and impersonal about this novel and it has its chief interest as a literary curiosity."* He states, however, very significantly, that Conrad took some pleasure in writing it, and himself said of it: "Strangely enough it is yet my share of 'Romance' that fills me with the least dismay."**

Conrad's instinct was right. *Romance* has not had its deserts. Anyone who picks it up will find it worth reading, and recognise Conrad's unmistakable touch so often that he will end by forgetting that Ford had any hand in it at all. Indeed, as I shall show, at least two-thirds of the book is Conrad's.

---

* J. Baines, *Joseph Conrad, a Critical Biography*, London, 1960, p. 277.
** Ibid., p. 275.

It is still a puzzle why a great writer, who had behind him such works as *The Nigger of the 'Narcissus'* and *Heart of Darkness*, should have joined forces with a beginner of incomparably less talent than his own. Ford, who was twenty-five years old as against Conrad's forty-three, had written short stories for the young, two books of verse, and the life of his grandfather, the Pre-Raphaelite Ford Madox Brown. Later on, indeed, Ford became a noteworthy author in his own right; but this still lay in the future. At the time that concerns us, he was a literary novice. He introduced into *Romance* an unoriginal adventure story called "Seraphina", of which he wrote the first draft. Conrad re-wrote it almost entirely, leaving only some of the original chapters.

Probably the main reason for Conrad's collaboration with Ford, at a time when Conrad himself was very little known, was his hope that the younger author, who was then beginning to be popular, would help him to catch the public fancy and make some money. The interests that the two men had in common must also have been a bond between them. Ford came from a family of artists, and, like Conrad, was a lover of French literature, and especially — again like Conrad — of Flaubert: he could talk for hours on matters of art. He lived in Kent, near Conrad and his family, to whom he let his house. The fact that Ford was only half-English (he had an English mother), and had lived more on the Continent than in England, may also have drawn him and Conrad together.

Whatever the reasons may have been, the two men decided to collaborate on a novel. Their first attempt, *The Inheritors*, was a failure, and the extent of Conrad's part in it is anyway insignificant. As early as 1898, however, they had an idea for a second novel, but it was not until 1900, just after Conrad had finished *Lord Jim*, that he set to work on *Romance*. The collaboration over it lasted two years, with breaks during which Conrad wrote works of his own. In 1902, *Romance* was ready for the printer. By comparison with Conrad's other books it did fairly well, although it failed to bring him the popularity he had hoped for.

At a quick reading, *Romance* is a typical adventure story in the manner of Robert Louis Stevenson — a succession of exciting events in an exotic setting. A young Englishman of good family, John Kemp, becomes involved against his will in smuggling and has to leave England for Jamaica, where a cousin of his has some property. From Jamaica — where he runs into more trouble — he is taken to the palace of a Spanish grandee in Cuba, near the

11. *Conrad w 1918 r.*

headquarters, in Rio Medio, of a gang of pirates led by an arch-villain and braggart, Manuel-del-Popolo. After the death of the old grandee, Don Baltazar Riego, Kemp escapes from the palace with the dead man's beautiful daughter, Seraphina, to save her from a worthless but powerful Irishman, O'Brien, who is scheming to win the hand and love of the beautiful heiress. During their escape, Seraphina and Kemp go through one hair-raising adventure after another, until, through O'Brien's machinations, they are parted by Kemp's final imprisonment. After innumerable tribulations, however, all ends well (a rare thing in Conrad, but introduced no doubt with an eye to popularity) with the union of the lovers in London, almost at the foot of the gallows that was to have sealed the hero's fate.

It is, as we see, a typical tale for the young, with a beautiful heroine, a dastardly villain, pirates, and so on. Such was the first idea — in Ford's "Seraphina". What did Conrad make of it? For there can be no doubt that most of *Romance* was by him. This is borne out by the extraordinary differences of style in the book, and by Conrad's own assertion that, of its five parts, the two central ones — the longest and most important — are almost entirely his work; that he collaborated in two others; and that only the first and last parts (the feeblest) were left unaltered from the first manuscript of "Seraphina".*

What did Conrad add to Ford's draft? To begin with, his use of words and his magnificent descriptions. The parts written by Ford are so colourless by comparison with Conrad's vivid and memor-able descriptions that we are never in any doubt as to the author-ship of any given passage. As soon as Conrad takes over, the stereotyped record of events turns into the almost palpitating reality of life. The descriptions — especially of scenery, seascapes, mists, storms, an attack by pirates on a ship — are unforgettable, and the emotional atmosphere is conveyed with the delicacy and subtlety of a great writer. Some pages of this unpretentious novel, written, so to speak, with the left hand, are among the best things that Conrad ever did.

The difference that Conrad made to Ford's lifeless draft cannot, of course, be explained only by the talent that brought to life everything it touched. There was a driving power behind this erup-tion of creative force. The superb descriptions and the convincing

---

* See Conrad's letter of 10 November 1923, to Ford: also the author's inscription on a copy of *Romance* in T. J. Wise's collection.

nature of the emotions portrayed are a sure sign of creative spontaneity — of Conrad's delight in this kind of "boy's story". Alongside the thinker, moralist and poet of the dramatic, there remained in Conrad, to the end of his life, and in spite of all his disillusionments, something of the boy who had left his own country in search of adventure on the high seas and in far-off lands. And it is in *Romance*, that "unimportant" story, that we see carried to the heights that Conrad never attained in any other work (with the possible exception of "youth"), that boyish, romantic side of nature, with its total and still youthful freshness and directness — a freshness and directness that are lacking in those later romantic works, *The Rescue* and *The Arrow of Gold* where the young man again spoke through the ageing writer. In *Romance* and "Youth" we find with greater understanding, what it was that drove Conrad for so many years over the high seas, before he crossed the disillusionment of the "shadow line".

But there was something else that contributed to the dash and free creative fantasy that we find in this book. Like his beloved Flaubert, he was an extremely conscientious writer, who made enormous demands on himself, and to whom writing was more of a penance than a joy. His letters say little of the delights of creation; they speak more often of its despair. This being so, we should give due weight to a remark of his that I have already quoted — that the writing of *Romance* "filled him with the least dismay".

Of course, the production of this boyish and seemingly trivial story — written, moreover, under the incognito of collaboration — did not burden him with the usual sense of responsibility. He felt almost as though he were on some light-hearted literary spree. And, when this relaxed sense of irresponsibility was on him, he was able to give more of himself, and to give it more lavishly, than in some of the books which seemed to him more important.

The only thing that can be urged against this delightful holiday mood was the fact that in *Romance* Conrad gave free rein to the exaggeration and melodrama that were so typical of his early creative period.

But even when engaged on such extravaganzas, Conrad was still pursued by the shadow that had haunted him ever since he exchanged his carefree youth for the troubled years of manhood. As I have mentioned, the two central and longest parts of the book ("Casa Riego" and "The Guitar and the Spade") were almost entirely by Conrad himself. And it is precisely in these two parts that we catch the tragic undertones of Conrad's voice — the Conrad for whom everything held a lurking grief. Among the many fictitious adventures of the novel, he brought in yet another drama of conscience — lightly sketched and introduced almost in parentheses, but in itself even more hopeless and insoluble than the one in *Lord Jim*.

Young Kemp, with a strict sense of honour that will not let him kill an unarmed man, spares the lives of two scoundrels who are at his mercy. They repay him by plunging both himself and — what he cares for much more — the woman he loves into an interminable succession of dangers and sufferings. Even the rascals themselves gain nothing from his magnanimity, for the deaths they later die are far more terrible than the death they escaped.

The section of the book that is entirely Conrad's work, and which casts its shadow over all the rest, is memorable not only for its glow of romantic adventure, but for the picture it gives of tragic results of honour and idealism — their futility: almost one might say, their dishonesty and selfishness. There seems to be no place, in this callous and knavish world, for either humanity or honour. Such things ruin not only those who lead their lives by them, but those whom these idealists most love; for such supposedly great qualities end up as credulous folly, or — even worse — as cruelty. It is indeed a kind of moral blind alley; however one behaves, whether well or ill, one cannot avoid error and guilt.

This theme is so integral, and recurs so often in the course of the story, that it is impossible to regard it as a subsidiary line introduced to heighten the interest of the plot. It is, moreover, taken up and expressed with penetrating clarity by Kemp himself, as he stands over the dead body of Manuel-del-Popolo, whose life he himself has so unwisely spared:

"I too had been human to that man. I had his life on the end of my pistol, and had spared him from an impulse that had done nothing but withold from him the mercy of a speedy death. This had been my pity.

"But it was Seraphina's cry — showing the stress and pain of the ordeal — that shook my faith in my conduct. It had brought over our heads a retribution of mental and bodily anguish like a criminal weakness. I was young and my belief in the justice of life had received a shock. If it were impossible to foretell the consequences of our acts, if there was no safety in the motives within ourselves, what remained for our guidance?".*

* *Romance*, p. 429.

Romance, then, or at least the central part of it, ends up as something very different from what Ford, and probably Conrad too, had first intended. So far from being a glorification of romantic youth it became an indictment of it; or one may say that it is both glorification and indictment, like the simultaneous accusation and defence of youth in *Lord Jim*. In *Lord Jim*, however, youth finally triumphs, although Jim is killed. Kemp survives, but the author gives him no other satisfaction, except that he regains Seraphina.

Pursuing the parallel between the two books, we see that *Romance* marks a transition from the drama of *Lord Jim* — who by human standards was to blame, although he atoned for his act — to the tragedy of absolute doubt: the tragedy of punishment without any preceeding guilt. This takes us straight into the hopeless world of *Nostromo*, and to the bitter statement in *A Personal Record*, that "love itself can wear at times the desperate shape of betrayal."

Thus Conrad in *Romance* seems to question even those moral values which he himself had always represented and defended. One could object, of course, that all this was an exercise of the imagination rather than an expression of the author's true emotional state, particularly as *Romance* was meant mainly as an entertainment; but even so it would show the direction in which Conrad's mind was moving at the time. Well might he say in a letter to Pinker, his literary agent; "This is not a boy's story".

RENDERING JUSTICE

There is in Conrad a rare passion for justice — an imperative need to look at every human problem, from all possible angles, and to render justice to everybody.

In the volume of *A Set of Six* we find a tale, brief but poignant in its cruel irony, about an anarchist *malgré lui* — a peaceful fellow, who through an unfortunate chain of circumstances falls into the clutches of real anarchists and comes up against the rigours of the law, which he has always respected and had no intention of breaking. The remarks that Conrad puts into the mouth of his hero, and certain comments of his own, show beyond any doubt the author's hatred of the idea of anarchy, whose only result can be to upset the already precarious equilibrium of the world, and to threaten, above all, the pathetic happiness of the very poor. On the other hand, Conrad makes a rich businessman utter anti-anarchistic platitudes so narrow-minded and unjust as to bring the opponents of anarchy into disrepute. Whatever his own judgement may be, Conrad always remembers the importance of hearing both sides.

In much the same way, we find, in *Under Western Eyes*, along-side the scathing indictment of Tsarist Russia, the contrapuntal theme of the shallow soullessness of "Western" Geneva. Another outstanding example is *Lord Jim*, where Conrad-Marlow, inspired no doubt by the same passion for the complete impartiality of justice, looks at the problem of his hero from diametrically opposed angles.

This characteristic of Conrad turns up in everything he wrote. His attitude to his fictional characters is essentially moral, not merely analytical or aesthetic. It is moral precisely as one's attitude to people in real life is moral. Conrad was not simply playing with his characters in his creative imagination; he felt under a moral obligation to them, and spared no pains to do them justice.

Once this is understood, it is easy to see the sincerity of what he says, in the "Author's Note" to *Under Western Eyes*: "I had never been called before to a greater effort of detachment: detachment from all passions, prejudices, and even from personal memories";* and the full significance of his declaration, in the preface to *The Nigger of the 'Narcissus'*, concerning "the attempt to render the highest kind of justice to the visible universe".**

What gave Conrad this extreme sensitiveness — one might almost say trauma — over justice? I think that a passage in his *Personal Record* throws light on the question: "The part of the inexplicable should be allowed for in appraising the conduct of men in a world where no explanation is final. No charge of faithlessness ought to be lightly uttered. The appearances of this perishable life are deceptive like everything that falls under the judgement of our imperfect senses."***

A sense of justice was no doubt inborn in Conrad. But anyone who, like himself, has had much to bear from the injustice and blindness of the accusations made against him, even by compatriots, will, to his dying day, shrink from judging anybody or anything irresponsibly. The sense of having suffered wrong goes deeper into the human soul than the most subtle refinements of conscience. And it was surely this sense that led to that fanatical feeling of justice that developed in Conrad.

---

* *Under Western Eyes*, p. VIII.
** *The Nigger of the 'Narcissus'*, p. VII.
*** *A Personal Record*, p. 35.

CONRAD'S POLISH COMPLEX: A FINAL DISCUSSION

Now, at the end, *audiatur et altera pars*. Of all the discussions I have had with Conrad scholars on the subject of his "guilt complex", I have chosen to quote an exchange of letters between Eloise Knapp Hay and myself. I did so because these letters bring out, with great clarity, our opposite points of view.

1.

Eloise Knapp Hay to Wit Tarnawski*

Dear Dr. Tarnawski,

Thank you for your interesting essay on *A Personal Record*. I hope you will accept the two enclosed manuscripts** as my answer, since they speak to some of the questions you raise.

You will see from the essay on Conrad's self-portraiture that I continue (as in my book) combating in everyone — including you! — the supposition that Conrad's art, in *A Personal Record* and elsewhere, is as you call it "defensive"; that we must interpret his agonies and reticences as primarily the result of some guilty feelings he suppresses instead of other, more personally felt, experiences he feels urged to *reveal*. In fact, focusing on the guilt complex always distorts the works in question (for me), though I think I'm as willing to see guilt complexes as the next reader when they appear to me really to be there — as in Melville and Kafka, for instance.

---

* Printed with the kind consent of the author.
** "Conrad's Self-Portraiture" and "Conrad between Sartre and Socrates".

Certainly the *question* of guilt — as a personal and universal question — was deeply disturbing to Conrad — and interesting. The *interest* of the question appears to me the cause of his recurrent uses of it, and of course it would not be interesting if it had not been personally important. I would not connect it with the so-called "guilt complex", however, because I think we must save the latter syndrome for cases of writers unable to objectify and act upon the gnawing worm of remorse that eats away at any sensitive conscience. Kafka's art generalised it but could not objectify it in the sense Conrad's *did*. Similarly Melville's characters in *Moby Dick, The Confidence Man* and *Pierre* make evil a general affliction in the face of which individuals are victimized, but never take hold of personal responsibility the way Conrad's art transcends neuroses (including the neurosis deriving from guilt feelings), while other modern writers who dealt with the same source of disease in the soul were incapable of transcending it. Again my response is my own — a matter of what I feel in reading.

The reason I wrote my paper on the self-portraiture is that Conrad's autobiography has always read more understandably to me as a maiden voyage into self-revelation than as an exercise in self-defence and evasion. I was therefore terribly excited to find in Conrad's letters to Methuen, Pinker and others (quoted in my paper) that Conrad's reasons for resisting self-revelation and then succumbing to outer and inner calls for such public exposure were part of a change that occurred both in his inspiration and in the public response to his writing after 1905. In fact, the reviews of *Nostromo* (one galling review by Garnett in particular) and the continuing efforts of Cunninghame Graham to draw Conrad into the Marxist-Russian orbit of European revolutions, added to the English infatuation (even in Bloomsbury) for everything Russian, seem to have provided the impulse. Until that moment, Conrad's natural reticence (in part simply good breeding) was intensified by his understandable impulse to appear as English as possible to readers who might otherwise view him as a freak. I do not share the view proferred by Orzeszkowa that Conrad might ever have written creatively in Polish. A man able to examine his own conscience sensitively (as you say he could) would never feel guilty for failing to do something he knew himself *incapable* of doing (as if he were to feel guilty for not having saved his father from dying). He might feel anguish over his helplessness but not guilt, properly defined.

The question of his "accounts with the past" is to me *the* important point, and I love your reference to his means of settlement

— some by payment, others by cancellation. I would say that the cancellation came through what he refused to discuss (the terms itemised by Orzeszkowa and those who had not known even who he was, like her). The payment (as his uncle never ceased to stress) came first in proving himself faithful to a good profession, a payment all the more acceptable because it was an international profession and he could prove that a Pole could work successfully up through the ranks. When this "payment" was succeeded by an even more impressive and more universal accomplishment, there could be no real question in a sensitive conscience that a narrow patriotism would have been a better form of payment.

The exhilaration he felt in finishing *Almayer's Folly*, as his letters to Marguerite Poradowska show, proved to him that he had found what was in him to do, and that it was good. This was a kind of payment in itself, to the world including Poland. Neither Kafka nor Melville ever expressed such relief from the burden of unworthy selfhood — and of course one of the first things he thought of was the account he thereby settled with all the "Shades" — his parents and uncle in particular. *Never does he speak at this point as if writing in Polish might be a question of conscience!* For him the past was a broader account.

Everyone knows that Poland gained more than it lost; that England gained no toadying immigrant but a new voice, speaking from within of things only an outsider could see and (as Ford and Orwell said) bringing the English into touch with things they had lost touch with. I doubt that Conrad felt any more guilt than Turgenev or James. His attention to themes of remorse and loyalty is not greater (apparently) than the attention of writers who never left Poland though he reaches deeper springs (as Mickiewicz did) by relating these themes to supranational loyalties. His betrayals never seem to be betrayals of a man's or woman's *native people but of a wider loyalty* (sometimes — as in *Under Western Eyes* — one that extends to an alien vision within one's own people). Thus the betrayal theme must be related to the question of loyalty irrespective of geographical boundaries (and language boundaries).

My interest in what I have written on the subject was to show that as late as 1905 Conrad was so concerned with muting the stress of his exotic origin that autobiography appeared to him a danger to his success as a writer. (Remember that this success was as he saw it part of his payment to the past). Hence the stress in *A Mirror* on his self-discipline in a worldwide profession, dominated by "the red ensign".

142

Only after finishing this half-revelatory book did the change in his readers' attitudes show him that his Polish past must have a more explicit place in his work. This change, as I see it, was more an *offensive than defensive* manoeuvre, on Conrad's part, I mean.

Yours sincerely

Eloise Hay

2.

Wit Tarnawski to Eloise Knapp Hay

Dear Mrs. Hay,

Thank you for the very interesting letter and the two enclosed essays. I regret that I am unable to send you my book on Conrad, which is just being translated into English. The book itself would be the best answer; your point of view needs the thorough presentation of another point of view; it cannot be fully discussed by my concentrating on particular items only. Nevertheless I will try to do my best and go through your arguments one by one.

First, a general remark. I see your point, but at the same time I cannot abandon mine, which is the result of many years of study of every aspect of Conrad's writings and life. I think that both are right in a way. Self-revelation does not exclude self-defence or evasion, and an offensive may be a means of defence. The final shape of an autobiography, as of any work of art, can never be the result of a single factor or of only one attitude. I am sure that a hidden guilt complex lingered on in Conrad, at least until he wrote *A Personal Record*, or perhaps even until Poland was liberated, although I agree with the distinction you make between the guilt complexes of Kafka and Conrad (Conrad being able to objectify his feeling of guilt and at last transcend it, and Kafka being its defenceless victim). That does not mean, however, that Conrad's guilt complex, even when overcome, did not recur and disturb him from time to time. Only the "absolution" (a religious term!) which came with the liberation of Poland swept it away completely — as we see from *The Rover*.

I agree that Conrad may not have bothered much about his neglected family and patriotic duties during the happy years of his sea-life (the "Youth" period). But when the gloom of the "shadow-line" engulfed him there is enough evidence to suggest that the ghosts of the past got hold of him. If one considers what Garnett wrote about Conrad's patriotic irritability in the Introduction to the *Letters of Joseph Conrad* ("the subject of Poland was painful to him, like pressing on a painful nerve"),* or Conrad's angry response to Orzeszkowa's accusation, it becomes obvious that he did not remain indifferent to the continuous charges of betrayal, or at least of neglect of his patriotic duties, brought against him by his compatriots — particularly as at that time, with the publication of his first novel, his previously inconspicuous private life had become a matter of public interest.

A feeling of social or national guilt or shame can certainly exist, even in defiance of one's own conviction. A man may be sure that he has done the right thing, and still feel guilty because he did not do what he was expected to do. A pacifist unwilling to go to war may join the Forces to avoid being called a coward. One should also remember the Novalis motto of *Lord Jim*, quoted by Conrad on many occasions, and showing clearly how sensitive he was to the opinion of other people. He could defy it, but he certainly felt it — especially when it was the opinion of his own coutrymen.

In spite of its crudeness and injustice, there was something in Orzeszkowa's accusation which hit Conrad hard. He did not forget it to the end of his life. In 1914, in Zakopane, he said to his cousin, Aniela Zagórska, when she gave him a novel by Orzeszkowa, "Don't even mention that hag to me. If you only knew... She wrote me such a letter once..." That was not a reaction to something that did not hurt.

We must remember that to leave one's country when it is oppressed or in danger is quite a different matter from leaving it when it is safe and free — as one might leave England or the United States. In the former case, one cannot help feeling a deserter, even if the reason for one's action was neither fear nor indifference.

You write that Conrad could not have felt guilty because there was no guilt involved. Well, I once had to leave my old mother in hospital. I was right to do so; I could not do otherwise. But immediately after I had left her I wrote a story about betrayal — and it was my feeling at the time that made me write it.

There is also the problem of the other, more subtle, desertion — Conrad's choice of a foreign language as the medium for his art.

* E. Garnett, *Letters from Conrad*, p. X.

Here again you say that Conrad would never feel guilty for failing to do something he knew himself incapable of doing. One can, of course, assume that for Conrad his only "desertion" was that of leaving Poland to become an English seaman, although in that case his feeling of guilt would be much more difficult to understand. His repeated insistence that he could write only in English sounds to me rather suspicious. Also unexplained is his unwillingness (overcome only by Garnett's persuasion) to write a second novel (*An Outcast of The Islands*) and thereby really cast in his lot as an English author, while the writing of a single novel (*Almayer's Folly*) might have been simply a seaman's whim. I have dealt more fully with this point in my study of *An Outcast*.

In your opinion the intrinsic interest of the question of guilt was a sufficient reason for Conrad's "recurrent use of it". I agree, that a purely intellectual curiosity in exploring all the aspects of fidelity and betrayal may have played an important part in Conrad's writing. I do not believe, however, that curiosity alone can create great works of art. In creative writing, general problems are usually evolved from personal ones; it is the personal memory that gives life and fire to the universal theme. Every artist's work has to have an emotional factor behind it. I am sure that this factor played a sub-stantial part in — as I call it — the "Lord Jim theme" in Conrad's books. He, like every writer, certainly exploited his own drama in his novels — inevitably being the observer as well as the victim of this drama. But the heart of the drama was, I firmly believe, personal.

Is it possible to imagine that the famous passage in *Lord Jim* about returning with a clear conscience to one's country, or the bitterness of the comment, in *A Personal Record*, on certain charges of desertion and faithlessness, could have been written "in cold blood", and purely as an exercise of the imagination or a piece of objective self-analysis?

I am afraid I have to stop. To sum up: in my opinion, neither intellectual interest nor the need for self-revelation (although both certainly played a part) was a sufficiently powerful motive for Conrad's recurrent, and indeed obsessive use, for so many of his creative years, of the themes of betrayal, desertion and guilt. We have, therefore, to accept the hypothesis of some kind of nagging remorse — especially if we recall that Conrad (as we know) could be a martyr to his own conscience.

Yours sincerely,

Wit Tarnawski

PART III

CONRAD THE EUROPEAN

A. Disillusion with Europe

THE SISTERS

1.

"The fabulous vastness of the country repeated itself day after day with the persistence of eternal truth — sank into the child's unconsciousness, coloured his childish thoughts, his young feelings, carried persuasion into his ignorance... Stephen, unwinking, looked on — smiled at immensity. In the day-time, from his mother's arms, he scrutinized with inarticulate comprehension the vast expanse of the limitless and fertile black-lands nursing life in their undulating bosom under the warm caress of sunshine. In the shallow folds of the plain dammed streams overflowed into an unruffled glimmer of small lakes, placid, as though soothed by the whispering tenderness of encircling reeds. On their banks dark willows and slim, unsteady birches stirred in the gentle and powerful breaths of the indolent steppe."*

Anyone who knows that part of the world will at once recognise the above as a description of what was formerly the Polish Ukraine, where Conrad was born. It used to be thought that the great artist of tropical landscapes had only once, in "Prince Roman", written about his native country. The discovery of *The Sisters*, from which I have quoted this passage, gave us descriptions that were even richer and more highly charged with emotion than anything in "Prince Roman".

I have used the word "discovery", for *The Sisters*, an unfinished novel, was until recently almost completely unknown to readers of Conrad.

The Sisters (Mursia, 1968), pp. 42-45.

It was published in 1928, after Conrad's death, as a text for bibliophiles, and the edition was limited to 926 copies. A Polish translation appeared in 1949 in the London weekly *Wiadomości*. The original text, and an Italian translation, were published simultaneously in 1968, by Ugo Mursia of Milan.

The fragment already quoted gives an idea of the very personal nature of the book. The picture of little Stephen taking in, for the first time, the sight of his native land, has the freshness and intimacy of the author's memories of his own past. In this unfinished work, the personal element lies everywhere on the surface; we cannot miss it. It may even be the reason for Conrad's having abandoned the book, when his artistic instinct suddenly warned him of the difficulty of finding a sufficiently objective form of expression for so personal a theme. Conrad, who began *The Sisters* in 1896, when he had finished *An Outcast,* soon abandoned it for the first draft of *The Rescue* (also left unfinished), and then for *The Nigger*, a work of an entirely different theme and mood.

To go back to the personal elements in *The Sisters*. The chief character, an artist called Stephen, was born, like Conrad, in the Ukraine, and the story of his artistic endeavours and disappointments might be an account of Conrad's own agonies during the early years of his literary career. The subject is all the more interesting in that the book was his first and last attempt to describe what an artist goes through in searching for perfection and his own means of expression. The fact that Stephen is a painter should not mislead us. Painting here stands for literature.

The second theme of *The Sisters*, the story of Rita, the young ward of the Ortegas, in whose house Stephen is living, also touched Conrad very closely. It is an echo of his romance in Marseilles with Rita Lastaola — a romance which must have left a deep mark on him, for he returned to it much later in *The Arrow of Gold. The Sisters*, however, differs entirely, in both concept and style, from this final version; although unfinished, it surpasses *The Arrow* in almost every way by its richness of subject and originality of expression.

Last but not least, in *The Sisters* we again catch undertones of Conrad's own drama concerning his family and nation — the drama familiar to us from so many of his works. The artist, Stephen, leaves his own country in pursuit of an illusory ideal of art; his parents, who stay behind, do not live to see his return. The passage in the novel in which Stephen learns of their death from his brother's letter again tells us what we already know so well in Conrad.

"Stephen, letter in hand, looked across space and time at the land of his birth. From afar it loomed up immense, mysterious — and mute. He was afraid of it. He was afraid of the silent dawn of life . . . Not there! Not there! . . . He wrote to his brother: 'I cannot return. You would not understand if I tried to explain. But, believe me, to return now they are dead would be worse than suicide, which is the unpardonable crime . . .' "* "Stephen remembered, could see, the pathetic faces of the dead who — he imagined — had died with his name on their lips. Defenceless, he was pierced by the venomous sharpness of remorse. He had abandoned those two loving hearts for the promise of unattainable things, for alluring lies, for beautiful illusions."**

This, like Marlow's speech in *Lord Jim* about returning to one's own country, is one of the passages in Conrad's writings which sounds like a passionate confession.

The personal — at times autobiographical — nature of *The Sisters* is evident even at the level of language. Nowhere else is Conrad's English so Polish in character. While working on the translation of this unfinished novel I sometimes felt that I was restoring to its original language something that had been translated into English.

2.

The Sisters appeared with a long introduction by Ford Madox Ford. Ford was a great admirer of this unfinished novel, which he saw as the presage of another Conrad, even more interesting and profound than the one we know. He writes in his Introduction: "Supposing that, at that parting of the ways in 1897, Conrad had chosen to write in French of the misty problems of the Slav soul . . . The vista that opens to me of the works of an immensely great international writer, another but more impassioned Turgenev, another Flaubert but more of a poet, has a gloomy glory that I cannot but regret. Contact with Anglo-Saxondom has, alas, a belittling effect on the artist, we so love trivialities and so avoid the contemplation of great causes."

Ford bewailed the fact that Conrad had abandoned the artistic and psychological theme of *The Sisters* for the seafaring *Nigger of the 'Narcissus'*. He ended with the sorrowful words: "Well, we should have had another Conrad . . . what a mysterious and gigantic figure that would have been, going away into the mists of the mind!"***

---

* *The Sisters*, p.53.
** Ibid., p. 50.
*** Ibid., pp. 29-30.

Ford certainly failed to appreciate Conrad's later work, and to realise that his love for the sea never lured him away from what he regarded as the greatest theme of all — man. For what, if not for his penetrating analysis of "the misty problems of the . . . soul", do we remember his greatest works — *Heart of Darkness, Lord Jim, Nostromo* and *Under Western Eyes?* But the very fact that Ford compared *The Sisters* with Conrad's magnificent later books is the best possible proof of how highly he valued this fragment.

Was his enthusiasm justified? He was certainly right in pointing out the unique place of *The Sisters* in Conrad's literary bequest, and in saying that some of its merits — or even some of its possibilities — were never to be found in Conrad again. But the question is whether we should regard it simply as an unfulfilled promise or, even in its present state, as a noteworthy achievement.

The fragment left to us is not a homogenous composition. The short text (50 pages) consists of three parts linked together quite loosely and differing both in the character of their contents and in artistic merit. Stephen's artistic Odyssey — which was udoubtedly the part of the book that aroused Ford's hopes that Conrad might decide to write of "the misty problems of the Slav soul" — was never more than an attempt, which, in this first draft, did not really come off. It has, indeed, the value of an interesting psychological and aesthetic document, but it is embarrassingly grandiloquent and exaggerated, and therefore — in spite of its obvious sincerity — unconvincing.

Grandiloquence and a tendency to pathos are, as we know, characteristic features of Conrad's early style, nowhere else is he so reminiscent of the worst romantic manner. The first fragment of the book is full of high-flown phrases about beauty, truth, exalted vocations, and the tragic destiny of the artist. It opens with the words: "If Stephen came from the East — if he possessed the inborn wisdom of the East — yet it must be said he was only a lonely and inarticulate Mage, without a star and without companions. He set off on his search for a creed — and found only an infinity of formulas. No angel's voice spoke from above to him."*

If we did not know that these words had been written by Conrad we might easily ascribe them to one of the nineteenth-century Romantics.

It is an entirely different matter when Conrad descends from aesthetic phraseology and the story of an artist's quest for beauty

---

* *The Sisters*, p.33.

(that quest which presents so many pitfalls to an inexperienced writer) and starts dealing with concrete reality. The story of Rita's childhood in the Basque mountains — the childhood of a wild young girl later adopted by a rich uncle — is remarkable for its psychological subtlety and the sharp-eyed realism of its descriptions of Rita's middle-class Parisian background. Everything here is alive, and not in the least hackneyed; one can almost feel Conrad's joy in setting out on this unexplored path. The style, too, in this section, is very much his own — vigorous, terse and tender by turns — entirely different not only from the ornate early style of *An Outcast*, but from what his style became when it was completely formed — a fact which confirms Ford's remark about the unpredictable possibilities of Conrad's talent. And although, as was almost inevitable in an unfinished work, his descriptions are either mere sketches or overloaded with detail, we can see at once that this part of the book was written by an artist whose power was already assured.

The same may be said of the third element in *The Sisters* — the story of Stephen's childhood and the village life of his parents. It is a small genre-painting, in which both the lyrical and the gently ironical passages are the work of a master. In general, wherever Conrad was able to look at the persons in his story from a distance, his touch had an astonishing certainty — astonishing, in view of the fact that this was, after all, only a sketch for a more mature work.

But we must not forget that it was only a sketch — a first draft, raw material — which would have undergone many stylistic alterations, and perhaps even — as sometimes happened in Conrad's works — a fundamental change of concept. The faults and inadequacies of the present text are largely due to its provisional character.

We have no means of knowing what form the completed book would have taken; we know only how rich it already is in style and content, despite its crudities and lack of finish. We must regret, with Ford, that *The Sisters* is incomplete.

3.

To those interested in Conrad, *The Sisters* is fascinating for yet another reason. It reveals a hitherto unsuspected aspect of the author's mind or, at least, a little-known period of his inner life.

We usually think of Conrad as having been implacably hostile to the Russian East, and of being himself an uncompromising representative and defender of the ideals of Western civilisation. This view of him is borne out by documentary evidence and by countless facts from his own life. He made his attitude quite clear by the title he gave to his novel about Russia — *Under Western Eyes*. One would think, from what is generally known of him, that his views had never changed — that ever since his childhood, on which Russia had left so lasting a scar, his attitude to all things Russian was one of unalterable suspicion and animosity.

The Sisters shows us that there were in fact fluctuations in his feelings. In this early novel, the Russian background is treated with indulgent irony — almost with affection. The artist, Stephen, a very attractive figure, is a Russian, although of Ukrainian origin. Stephen's wanderings across Western Europe in search of beauty and truth end in total disillusionment. It is not the East — not Russia — that comes under fire in *The Sisters*; it is Western Europe. Life in the West horrifies the young artist by "the interior jumble of its variegated littlenesses... There was nothing great because all was very finite, definite, bound to the earth. On the other side... there was the august world of the infinite, the Eternal... always hopelessly remote from those unquiet hearts in which its mystery could awake nothing but secret fear, or more secret scorn."*

When his brother appeals to him to return, Stephen replies, "You are right. There is no country like our country and no people like us — peasants. We are God's children." Finally, writing in his own person, the author contrasts "the inborn wisdom of the East" with the clearly defined but terribly narrow limits of Western thought.

The subjective nature, emphasis and obvious sincerity of the first part of *The Sisters*, from which I have taken the above passages, leave no room for doubt that Conrad's views on Russia, expressed by the narrator in his second "Russian" novel, *Under Western Eyes*, written fifteen years later, had undergone a radical change since he wrote Stephen's story. The above title could almost be used for *The Sisters*, with the alteration of one word — "Under *Eastern* Eyes".

The Sisters was written two years after Conrad had left the merchant navy to settle in England and devote himself to literature. It is the first of several works that he wrote at that time —

---

* *The Sisters*, pp. 35-6.

"The Return", "Karain", and, above all, *Heart of Darkness* — which show his deep disillusionment when, after sailing the seven seas for many years, he returned to his native Europe. There were, at the time other factors at work, such as his friendship with the Garnetts, who were enthusiastic over Russia, and his introduction, through them, to Russian literature. This may have influenced him, but it seems to have been chiefly his recent experience of the conventional civilisation of Europe that caused him to react against it so strongly that even Russia — simply by being unlike the West — appeared in a more attractive light. Memories of the simple, natural life in his native Ukraine (whose local and Russian elements were by then inextricably intermingled); the "wide Russian soul" compared with the limitations of Western civilisation; the recurrent spell exercised on the roving sailor by the "inborn wisdom of the East"; one may even say, Rousseau's old ideal of the child of nature, the uncorrupted savage — all this came suddenly to the surface, soothing his burning sense of grievance, and causing the *salto mortale* which led to the writing of *The Sisters*. We may also recall the sympathetic young Russian in *Heart of Darkness*.

It is only when we know this phase of his attitude to Russia that we can appreciate the hard mental work that Conrad put into the fifteen years that lay between *The Sisters* and the writing of his great novel about Russia — only then that we can see how carefully he must have weighed the arguments on both sides before declaring himself on the side of the "narrow" West, with all its limitations, against the fascination of the Eastern immensity. Seen in this light, his return to the anti-Russian attitude that first appeared in his famous "Autocracy and War" (1905), and later found unforgettable expression in *Under Western Eyes*, no longer seems a predominantly emotional reaction, born of racial and personal resentment against Russia, but the outcome of a mature reconsideration of two conflicting views — a thoughtful and deliberate choice.

4.

The better to understand Conrad's change of attitude to the East-West problem we should bear in mind one of the predominant features of his mentality. Its elements were very well balanced; his exceptionally wide mental range and his ability to see every side of a subject went with a gift for making practical decisions. As a rule, the more possibilities one sees, the harder it is to make up one's mind between them. Hamlets are born of such a state of mind. But Conrad was always able to choose. This may be explained by the fact that, thinker and poet though he was, he had, for twenty years, stuck to a hard and eminently practical profession, which called for a swift and definite decision in an emergency. To this may be added a feature characteristic of Conrad — that all the decisions, to which I shall here refer, had a moral aspect and purpose: the protection and integrity of man's soul.

Let me give one example. Although his view of the world was essentially pessimistic, and he saw neither purpose nor meaning in the way it was conducted, he accepted, for himself and his heroes, a simple and straightforward moral programme, devised precisely by people who believed in purpose and meaning. He accepted this programme, not because it was philosophically unassailable, but because it worked from a practical point of view, and saved men from being destroyed by material or moral disaster.

To take another example. Conrad, himself a revolutionary by both family tradition and his own psychological bent — the avowed enemy of all tyranny, and bitterly derisive of capitalistic material interests — was, socially and politically, a supporter of the established order rather than a believer in revolution and violent change. He chose the lesser of two evils, preferring an imperfect order to social upheavals which release the worst elements in man and often put humanity on an even lower level than the one from which it was trying to raise itself.

As regards the choice with which we are here most concerned, Conrad, clearly though he saw the materialism, formalism and spiritual narrowness of the West, nevertheless took his stand on the side of Western legality, respect for individual rights, and conventional morality against Eastern extremism, tyranny, contempt for law, and lack of moral standards. As I have tried to show, his choice was neither quick nor easy. He had a long way to go and a hard mental and moral battle to fight before he finally decided to throw in his lot with the side which, although itself far from perfection, was better suited to the imperfect nature of man.

"THE RETURN"

"The Return", one of the stories in *Tales of Unrest*, finds no favour with the critics. It holds, nevertheless, an important place in Conrad's writings, if only because it was his first and most uncompromising indictment of Victorian England.

It was not written all at once. Conrad finished the greater part of it in the spring of 1897, then laid it aside, and did not take it up again until he had completed *The Nigger of the 'Narcissus'* in the autumn of the same year, when he added a few pages.

The hero of "The Return" is Alvan Hervey, an Englishman in good society, who believes implicitly in his own perfection and that of his circle, and that this perfection depends mainly on one thing — keeping up appearances. On returning home one evening, he finds a letter from his apparently irreproachable wife, who tells him that she is leaving him for the editor of a "society paper" financed by Hervey himself. But before he has time to collect his thoughts and find some way out of this humiliating situation, his wife returns; her courage has failed her, for, like her life's companion, she puts the conventions of her little world far above any emotional impulse.

Hervey, his self-confidence restored, subjects his wife to lofty tirades and moralisings on the evils of abandoning one's duty, until he reduces her to a state of hysteria and makes her again decide to leave him.

This, of course, Hervey cannot allow, for to him the only thing that matters is to keep up appearances. He insists on her having dinner with him as usual, so that everyone, including the servants, may think that nothing unusual has happened.

But his wife, who shows herself to be an apt pupil, plays her part so well, and is so calm and self-possessed during dinner, that Hervey is alarmed by this impenetrable dignity that may be hiding anything, without giving him the least clue as to what his wife is really thinking and feeling. The man who believes in appearances is caught in his own trap.

The ending (only a few pages of which may have been added in the autumn of 1897) has little in common with the ironical concept of what has gone before, and is psychologically somehow at odds with it.

A few outspoken words from his wife, who suddenly says that he has never loved her, make Hervey realise that a life without love and trust is not worth living. He tries to persuade himself that behind his wife's enigmatic silence lay just these gifts of trust and love. But his attempt to embrace her is repelled with horror; he sees his mistake, and that it is useless to look for love from her, who could not even bring herself to go away with her lover. Hervey realises that he cannot go on living with a woman who does not love him — a woman whose feelings he will never know, and whom he can no longer trust. Moreover, all that he has just been through has aroused his conscience, and he begins to see his life in a new light. He asks his wife if she can live without love and trust; when she says that she can, he cries out, "Well, I can't!" and leaves the house, never to return.

This sudden conversion of the hero — this moral crisis in the life of a man hitherto presented as a heartless egoist, snob and hypocrite — is utterly at variance with all his previous behaviour, and suggests a puppet artificially brought to life.

We must remember that the last pages of "The Return" were written after a long break. In his "Author's Note" to the collection of stories in which "The Return" appears, Conrad speaks of the difficulty that he had in writing it, and of the "disillusion" that it caused him. It seems likely that at some point he was held up by the problem of finding a suitable ending, and for this reason laid it aside for half a year. When he went back to it, he completely altered the ending in both tone and conception.

In the first, and decisive, part of the story, Hervey is shown as a ruthless egoist, to whom only two things matter — his own interest, and what people think of him. Any discrepancies between these two basic — and often opposed — principles, he reconciles by hypocrisy. He gives this hypocrisy the high-sounding name of self-restraint, and makes it an ideal in his life. But every truth — and the deep emotions that reveal truth — is outlawed as base and shameful.

158

For at least the first ninety pages, Conrad writes of his "hero" with open irony and dislike, as a few quotations will show. "...Men and women who feared emotion, enthusiasm or failure more than fire, war or mortal disease... Like the men he respected they could be trusted to do nothing individual, original or startling — nothing unforeseen and nothing improper... Self-restraint is everything in life, you know. It's happiness, it's dignity... it's everything... Crime may be forgiven... but passion is the unpardonable and secret infamy of our hearts, a thing to curse, to hide and to deny; a shameless and forlorn thing that tramples upon the smiling promises, that tears off the placid mask, that strips the body of life... that ugliness of truth which can only be kept out of daily life by unremitting care for appearances... The ideal must, must be preserved — for others, at least."*

In a letter to his friend Garnett, Conrad calls the hero of "The Return" "a beastly bourgeois", but Hervey is not a bourgeois in the international sense; one might not find his equivalent abroad. He is distinctively English — a Victorian Englishman in good society, with all the stiffness, snobbery and hypocrisy typical of his class — a man such as Conrad must often, over the years, have come across in London.

"The Return", written during his fourth year in England, shows how hard he found it to adapt himself to his new surroundings, and to accept the psychology, when at home, of the race whose prowess at sea he had so often extolled. "The Return" was written when Conrad was a close friend of the critic, Garnett, and already on good terms with many other English intellectuals; but simultaneously his dislike of the whole breed of Herveys smouldered within him, until, in this story, it suddenly blazed forth.

Perhaps, to the end of his life, he never quite shook off the Anglophobia with which his early years in England had inspired him. Many of the English characters in his books, from Donkin in *The Nigger of the 'Narcissus'* to the Fyne family in *Chance*, are presented with biting irony. But nowhere else did his dislike of certain characteristics of the nationality he had adopted burst out quite so violently as in his portrait of the "exemplary" Hervey.

In fact, the very fury of this outburst may explain the totally unexpected and unconvincing rehabilitation of Hervey. Conrad may

---

* *Tales of Unrest*, pp. 120 ff.

have suddenly felt that he was overdoing the irony and letting himself be carried away by his dislike of his principal character. Perhaps he did not want, at the beginning of his literary career, to offend his English readers. Or, with his innate sense of justice, he may have wanted to say something in favour of the "beastly bourgeois" — to find some human value, even in him. But this is simply guess-work. The only thing we can be sure of is that the change is unconvincing and does not help the story.

However, as I have already said, "The Return" does not deserve the cool reception given to it by the critics. It should be read by every lover of Conrad. The concept of driving the hero into the trap of his hypocrisy is excellent, and the psychological portrait of him is both accurate and scathing. Moreover, the atmosphere and subtle psychological analysis give the story a unique place among Conrad's works. Finally, "The Return" is an important landmark in the history of his inner life and adaptation to his new environment.

But it must be admitted that the story as a whole does not come off. Nor is this solely due to the change of concept and the psychological inconsistency discussed above. "The Return" is unsuccessful in tone, style and artistic method. At this early stage of his career, Conrad was still feeling his way as an artist, and although at times he triumphantly found it, there were other times when he failed completely.

His failures were usually due to a kind of baroque extravagance — an over-indulgence of his powers of expression. Exaggeration is a feature of all his Malayan novels — *An Outcast*, "Karain" and the early part of *The Rescue* — but it suits the tropical background better than the English one, where it has less artistic justification. In the grey London scene it is particularly out of place.

Yet it is precisely against this background in "The Return" that exaggeration is heightened to an almost unbearable extent. In this story covering a few hours, and spun out to nearly a hundred pages, everything is overdone — the emotional quality of the metaphors, the minute detail and inordinate length of the descriptions, the emphasis laid on the most obvious truisms. Moreover, Conrad attributes to his cold and very ordinary hero his own depth of feeling and far-ranging vision, as though, in this way at least, he wanted to make up to this City gentleman for the drab dullness that was so stifling after the rich colour and elemental passions of Conrad's Malayan heroes.

Everything in the book shows how hard it must have been for Conrad, at least in those early years, to fit into the limitations of conventional society in Victorian England, and accept, for his art, the stereotyped conformity of the Europen novel of his day.

All this comes out most strikingly — and, artistically, most disastrously — in "The Return"; but we see it in everything that he wrote at the time. The restrictions imposed by the objective realism that Conrad admired in Flaubert and Maupassant seem to have irked him almost past endurance. Lyrical passion and a running commentary appear in his descriptive prose wherever it is possible for him to squeeze them in, however incongruously. The emotionalism, imagination and experience that he had hoarded under the self-imposed silence of his twenty years at sea, now dominated every character and situation of which he wrote.

Only against this background can we understand the origin of Marlow, who appears for the first time in "Youth" (1898). Conrad could not find detachment and artistic equilibrium until he had introduced into his work this rambling narrator, on whom he laid the excess weight of his own creative ballast — his observations, his unrest, and his ponderings over the mystery of existence.

"KARAIN"

In *Tales of Unrest*, the early collection of Conrad's short stories which also contains "The Return", it is "Karain" which undoubtedly dominates all the others by its originality, power of expression and richness of artistry.

In one respect it is an undoubted masterpiece. Conrad here applied, with a truth and allusive power that he never surpassed, the technique of reminiscence which was to become an essential feature of his writings. It was, no doubt, with full deliberation that he sub-titled the story "A Memory". It starts off with a spate of characters, faces and voices — all at first quite indistinguishable, and which appear in the author's memory against the background of a tropical landscape. From this crowd there gradually emerges the figure who is to become the hero — Karain. This extra-ordinarily faithful rendering of a process of dreamy reminiscence has such evocative power that the reader becomes involved in the drama unfolding before his eyes as though it were part of his own memories. This of course is also the result of the author's fascinated absorption in his subject.

In the "Author's Note" to *Tales of Unrest*, Conrad tells us that the subject is almost identical with that of "The Lagoon", a story in the same collection, which also describes an act of betrayal involving two people who are very close to each other. But, he adds, "the idea underlying it was quite different". What was this "idea"?

I shall not here insist on Conrad's obsession, in both these stories, with the theme of betrayal. I have said enough on the subject elsewhere. What, however, at once strikes one in "Karain" and, by its intensity, puts it in quite a different category from "The Lagoon", is the author's state of enchantment with the glowing world of the tropics and the moral health of its people.

In the same "Author's Note", Conrad also tells us that he started writing "Karain" on a sudden impulse as soon as he had finished *The Nigger of the 'Narcissus'* and while he was writing "The Return". He adds that this was the only time when he "tried to write with both hands at once, as it were".

We can well understand this impulse. We feel that "Karain" was an outlet for the imagination and emotions — an escape from all that Conrad was depicting with such revulsion in "The Return": the City of London and its respectable but soulless inhabitants. "Karain" begins and ends with two contrasting and unforgettable visions. It opens with one of Conrad's most marvellous descriptions of a tropical landscape, the background inseparable from the dignified Karain; and it ends with a picture of unparalleled ugliness and inhuman congestion in a London street. The writer ends his story with the words: "It is there; it pants, it runs, it rolls; it is strong and alive; it would smash you if you didn't look out; but I'll be hanged if it is yet as real to me as . . . as the other thing . . . say, Karain's story."*

And it is in these final words, this rejection of the present horrible reality in favour of the glories of memory and the enchantment of dreams, that we find the "idea" of which Conrad speaks in his "Author's Note" — the idea behind the story, and the impulse that brought it into being. Conrad had had enough of shore-life and of Europe. His whole nature looked back longingly at the wonderful past — the sea he had left, the distant lands he had visited on his voyages, and the simple, honest people he had known and loved.

---

* *Tales of Unrest*, p. 55.

A SUMMING-UP

To sum up. From the time when, after twenty years of wandering in the company of unsophisticated seamen, or among the simple-hearted inhabitants of exotic countries, Conrad, in 1893, renewed his contact with Europe, the self-satisfied nonentity of civilised man struck him all the more forcibly by its contrast to what he had seen on his voyages. His visit to the Congo had already opened his eyes to the "horror" of civilisation; and his subsequent prolonged stay in England made civilisation still more hateful to him. From *The Sisters* onwards, he attacked this horror, contrasting, in *The Sisters*, the effete, empty and corrupt West with the wisdom and simplicity of the East, or with the childlike, ignorant but profound integrity of the Malays (in "Karain" and "The Lagoon"); and, finally, exposing, in "The Return", the moral baseness of Victorian hypocrisy.

But it was in *Heart of Darkness* that he finally achieved what he had set out to do. There he led the "white pilgrims" into the wilds, cut the familiar ground from under their feet, showed up their inner void by putting them to the annihilating test of barbarism and lawlessness, and, by this final stroke, destroyed the monster that had made his first years on land so hateful to him.

After *Heart of Darkness* he returned to his attack on the golden calf of civilisation, here represented by the "material interests" in *Nostromo*. The atmosphere is different; he writes with less passion and more subtlety, and his range is wider; but the result is even more shattering.

There is an obvious resemblance between the themes of these two works which show his outlook on the modern world. Costaguana reminds us of Africa — an Africa softened, to some extent, by civilisation. The silver in Costaguana has the same disruptive effect on men's characters as gold and ivory have in Africa — except that, in Costaguana, it does not act with such devastating swiftness.

After so many years of homeless wandering, Conrad's bitter disillusionment with his native Europe must have come as an unexpected blow to him, and completed the process of estrangement and isolation which later became the main theme of his books. Moreover, the spiritual recluse that he now was, became engaged in a new conflict, later described in *Lord Jim* — a conflict with himself, in which he began to question his own worth. He found the answer to this general upheaval of things around and within him in "a very few simple ideas" on which, as he tells us, the world rests, and to which he afterwards clung with desperate determination.

B. A Final Settlement of Accounts with Russia

UNDER WESTERN EYES TODAY

1.

What most strikes the contemporary reader of *Under Western Eyes* is the fact that a novel written over seventy years ago, by a man long dead, should still retain its political relevance. In fact, it is only now, when we have come to know more about Soviet Russia, that we can do justice to this tale of Russia under the Tsars.

The story of Razumov's denunciation of his colleague is repeated endlessly, in a hundred different forms, throughout the length and breadth of Russia today. It is such denunciations that give the State its inconceivable hold over all its subjects. Mikulin's seemingly harmless conversations with Razumov are a foretaste of the nocturnal sessions with the KGB that end in the total breakdown of their victims. The first part of the book, especially, gives so penetrating and comprehensive a picture of the reality of Russian affairs, and keeps so astonishingly close to the present features of Russian life, that it compares, in depth and illuminating force, with the best that has lately been written to throw light on the murky happenings behind the Iron Curtain.

I would go even further and say that Conrad's novel holds pride of place among the very best of such books; in many ways it has not, even seventy years later, been improved on, for it contains elements of lasting value that have been ratified by time.

It is, to begin with, a piece of literary pioneering. Even its title — *Under Western Eyes* — has a certain historical significance.

Conrad was surely the first fiction-writer in Europe to show so clearly and with such assurance the complete separateness and strangeness of the Russian East — to draw so firm a line of demarcation between Russian psychology and Western. His revelations are now truisms. But in 1911, when the novel was published, it took genius to write a book about a humble English teacher of languages who watched, with growing bewilderment, the treachery, moral anarchy and childish pride of the Russian soul. The fact that Conrad came from a country where, for centuries, East and West had rubbed shoulders with each other — a country that had seen the danger of Russia long before Western Europe was alive to it — gave him both a deeper feeling for Western values and a penetrating insight, free from illusions, into the spirit of Russia.

Moreover, the truths that Conrad made known concerning the Russian soul and Russian affairs had this advantage over the discoveries made today, that they show the amazing change-lessness of the elements that have shaped Russian history. Peter the Great and Stalin, the Ochrana* and the Cheka, are very much alike except in name; the change, if there is any, lies in the perfecting of the instrument. The author himself points this out at the end of his "Author's Note", where he speaks of "the truth of the saying that the tiger cannot change his stripes nor the leopard his spots".** The very fact that Conrad's revelations, dating from so far back, are in such extraordinary agreement with those made today, opens far wider horizons than any in contemporary writings on Russian affairs, and makes us question the hope that some essential change may take place in that "corrupted, dark im-mensity".

Another advantage that Conrad had over present-day experts on Russian affairs lay in his refusal to be carried away by what was happening at the moment, and his determination to concentrate on the essence of events rather than on their immediate, un-doubtedly ominous, but not always essential form. Being far-sighted and detached, and, moreover, a psychologist, moralist and observer "of the soul of things" he noted above all the psycho-logical and moral properties of the Russian character, in which he detected elements which today, when the main emphasis is on the political and ideological aspect, may remain obscured.

---

* Ochrana — the secret police of the Tsarist regime.
** *Under Western Eyes*, p. X.

How provocative of thought, for instance, is Conrad's insistence on the homelessness of Razumov, whom he deliberately deprives of all family and social ties, seeing in this deprivation a major cause of Razumov's lack of moral stamina and servile acceptance of the idea of tyranny. Soviet power depends on man's being homeless — cut off by all possible means from family, class and religion — since only a rootless man, without ties, can be turned into a pitiless and unfailing tool of the State.

But the most unusual quality in Conrad's novel lies in something entirely different — his quiet, disciplined but impregnable certainty of his own position. Almost all the contemporary descriptions and analyses of Soviet Russia — even those that are the most anti-Communist — lack this note of calm certainty: there is always an undertone of fear of Russia's hidden might, often some doubt of the political and moral power of the West, and even a subconscious admiration of the adversary.

Conrad came of another generation — a generation that was not under the spell of Communist Russia's successes, and that still believed firmly in its own cause. This might not have been enough, if Conrad's attitude had not had the backing of a strict moral and intellectual code, which he contrasted with the cynical falsity and moral corruption of the East.

It is Conrad's confidence in his own position, in the ground on which he had taken his stand and from which he formed his judgements, together with his astonishing awareness of all the weaknesses of his opponent, which makes *Under Western Eyes* such a remarkable book.

It must not be forgotten that all these merits of the novel are due to the painstaking and disciplined thought and study that Conrad put into it — few works of art have had so much. As he himself wrote at the time to John Galsworthy, "I am trying to capture the very soul of things Russian".*

The central figure, on whom Conrad focuses his attention throughout, is of course Razumov. On one occasion Razumov cries "I am it (i.e. Russia)" and this was most probably meant by the author to be more than a dramatic exclamation. Conrad made Razumov the principal actor in the drama; it was chiefly in *his* soul that Conrad tried to "capture the very soul of things Russian". This is why I propose to comment briefly on Razumov.

---

* January 6, 1908.

The characteristic that Conrad most wanted to bring out in the student Razumov was his moral immaturity, not to say his complete lack of moral sense. He betrays his colleague, Haldin, without a qualm — in fact, with the feeling that he is doing his duty. It is, as I have said, this lack of moral standards that makes him so useful and willing a tool of the autocracy that demoralizes everything it touches. Razumov himself was an indispensable part of the system. Without the Razumovs there would have been no Tsars.

The author's intention seems clearly defined by what he says about Razumov at the beginning of the book, where we see him as a student chiefly concerned with his forthcoming examination and subsequent position in life: he is, at least at the beginning of the story, "an ordinary young man" with "an average conscience" — and, as the author makes clear, a careerist. His later hatred of revolution is not ideological; it is the result of circumstance; before the crisis over Haldin, he had flirted with free-thinking. He begins to hate revolution because it complicates his own life; later he becomes inextricably entangled in the net of autocracy, and hates revolution more than ever, as the cause of all his misfortunes. His "ideology" is born of the threat to himself, and of his haunting sense of homelessness — the waif-like condition that has to have some external strength to lean on. On the Russian steppe, where a merciless wind is blowing, one can walk either with it or against it. Razumov was not a Haldin.

Conrad does not, however, deprive Razumov of all moral feeling. Callous and committed to a life of treachery as he is, Razumov is continually haunted by spectres and subjected to mental torment — which cannot be attributed only to his constant fear of being found out.

The better to understand what was in Conrad's mind, we should compare Razumov's case with the short story "Karain" (*Tales of Unrest*). The story describes the remorse of an uncivilised man who has killed his friend. He, like Razumov, is pursued by phantoms — the ghost of the murdered man appears to him even in the daytime; but that is all. He says nothing to suggest that he feels any scruples over what he has done. The same is true of Razumov. Until his love for the sister of the colleague he betrayed causes his psychological breakdown, he has no sense of guilt or conscious remorse, nor does he ever connect his inner unrest and the visions which torment him with the thought of his terrible act.

In both men — the Malay and Razumov — the workings of conscience take place in the subconscious; the human mind and will play no part at all.

To Conrad, who, during his voyages, had learnt much about the psychology of primitive races, Razumov was an example of moral primitivism — an unenlightened morality like that of Karain, co-existing with the fully developed mentality of the civilised.

Even Razumov's public confession to the revolutionaries — a typically Russian psychological reaction — has not the mark of an entirely deliberate moral act. It is rather a sudden, unexpected outburst from some unknown depths of his soul.

While Conrad was writing *Under Western Eyes*, he seems to have asked himself whether, in the savage and cynical Russian world that was so utterly alien to him, there was, after all, some sensitiveness and moral responsibility. With his deep faith in human values all over the world he did not give a negative reply. He therefore endowed Razumov, in spite of his apparent amorality, with a sort of subconscious conscience, which troubles and haunts him and at last produces a complete change of moral attitude which — but only at the very end — assumes the character of a consciously accepted psychological process.

This kind of morality, however, is a very uncertain safeguard. We have only to think what would have become of Razumov if he had not, quite by chance, met Natalia Haldin. The secret police would have had yet another loyal agent.

In his "Author's Note" Conrad says that "Razumov is treated sympathetically". It would be more accurate to say that he is treated with understanding. All that Conrad writes about his strange hero strikes a cold and often ironic note. It is true that, as the book goes on and Razumov's character changes, Conrad's own attitude changes as well. The spiritual torment of Razumov, roused from moral apathy by his love for Haldin's sister, is treated without that note of irony with which, at the beginning, Conrad described the anguish of the trapped egoist. But right up to the end of the book there is some shadow of disapproval, some un-acknowledged barrier between Razumov and the author. Even the exaggerated and bombastic style of Razumov's written confession is a sign of Conrad's distaste for this sort of breast-beating. But most telling of all is the way the novel ends. The challenge that Lord Jim throws to fate during the final test ends triumphantly

Conrad in 1920.

with his fearless death: Razumov's challenge leads to his degrading mutilation. These unstated differences tell us more of the author's attitude to the matter than any explicit verbal formulation could do.

Conrad understood, but did not seem able — in the person of his teacher of languages — to forgive. To Conrad with his deeply moral nature and vast sense of responsibility, Razumov, egoistic, and, for much of the time, without any sense of moral responsibility, did not seem fully human, as Conrad understood humanity.

The novel contains many sharp notes of irony or contempt relating to the other characters in the Russian community in which Razumov lives, but the pity with which Conrad regards his central character — a pity wholly lacking in respect — is perhaps the most significant expression of his critical judgement, and his repudiation of the spirit of Russia.

2.

There has been some serious criticism of the artistic aspect of *Under Western Eyes*. One is bound to admit that from that point of view the novel has its obvious weaknesses. Taken, however, as a whole it is a major work of art — one of the most remarkable books written by Conrad. The first and last parts are undoubtedly works of consummate art — particularly the first part, with its concision and clarity, and the truth of its picture of the Tsarist Russia of those days. The last part, too, in which Conrad in the setting of "Western" Geneva, returns to "the very heart of things Russian", has passages of great artistic power. The scene, in Laspara's house, describing Razumov's confession and humiliation, is one of the most powerful pieces of writing ever achieved by Conrad.

Compared with these two genuinely "Russian" parts, where Conrad is at his best, the middle of the book, describing Russian revolutionaries in the international society of Geneva, seems superficial and rather stereotyped. There is also a marked slowing-down of the narrative. But even these less successful parts extend the picture of revolutionary Russia, and — more importantly — show the change gradually taking place in Razumov's subconscious mind; without this gradual change, the crisis in Part Four would come as a complete *volte face*. The central parts are, then, necessary.

Moreover, this slowing down of the action in the middle of the book has a purpose and logic of its own; it is the formal equivalent of the emergence of a new man in Razumov. The author suspends the action because everything in the hero is in a state of suspension, and there is no knowing which way things will go. One may contest the advisability of this solution, but one cannot deny the originality of the concept.

Under Western Eyes is, then, an outstanding achievement not only intellectually but artistically, and takes its place alongside *Lord Jim* and *Nostromo* as a *tour de force* of fictional form.

"THE SECRET SHARER"

It is characteristic of Conrad as a writer that in many of his books he returns to the same problems and examines them from a new angle. Among these different concepts we find one which may be called an explanatory variation on a basic theme. These concepts occur in works of minor importance, usually written immediately after one of his great books, on the central idea of which they throw more light by providing a contrasting solution. One example among others is "The Lagoon" from *Tales of Unrest*: here Conrad contrasts the Malay's honest, noble reaction to a shameful deed in his past with the irresponsible and evasive behaviour of the white man in *An Outcast of the Islands*.

To me, "The Secret Sharer" seems much the same sort of illuminating pendant to *Under Western Eyes*. In "The Secret Sharer" — written, significantly, at the same time (1909) as *Under Western Eyes* — we are shown a totally different reaction on the part of the hero to the almost identical situation in the scene between Razumov and Haldin (after which Razumov betrays Haldin to the police). In both cases the fugitive, who has committed a murder, takes refuge with another man. In both, there is a certain bond between the involuntary host and his visitor: in *Under Western Eyes*, both men are students; in "The Secret Sharer", both are seamen. To make the similarity closer, in both cases the fugitive, under mounting tension, takes on a spectral appearance to the host. That the parallel was deliberate seems obvious.

In "The Secret Sharer" Conrad shows us how he thought a decent man would behave in such circumstances. The captain in "The Secret Sharer" felt an instinctive human bond with the runaway from the first moment of their meeting — and, at the same time, a personal responsibility for his uninvited guest. This sense of fellowship and comradeship, and of his own obvious duty to help, was quite spontaneous; no further reason was needed than that one man was in trouble and had thrown himself on the mercy of another. Conrad carries this thought to an even higher point of tension, and stresses it, with unusual insistence, throughout the whole course of the action, as the chief and most important theme of the story. It should be noted that in "The Secret Sharer" the fugitive's act was much less admirable, much less deserving of help, than Haldin's, and that the comradely bond between the two men was far less close: but in the short story it is the situation itself that tightens the human bond — a bond so natural, so instinctively felt, as to need no explanation or justification.

"The Secret Sharer" is a tribute to comradeship — even the comradeship imposed by unforeseen circumstances; it is, at the same time, a condemnation of Razumov, with his appalling, inhuman lack of comradely feeling, where one might have expected it to be almost automatic, since Haldin had deliberately put himself in his power, whereas in "The Secret Sharer" it is sheer chance that guides the swimmer to the ship. Moreover, the swimmer was an unknown seaman, not a colleague from the same university.

Another interpretation of "The Secret Sharer" — a psychoanalytic one suggested by eminent Conrad scholars such as A. J. Guerard and D. Hewitt — has recently been gaining widespread support. According to this theory, the theme of the tale is the duality of the human personality — the lurking presence of a secret, darker self in everyone. Hence the title "The Secret Sharer".

One interpretation, however, need not exclude the other. A work of art not infrequently lends itself to several interpretations, which may indeed reflect the complex intentions of the author. My only concern is to show that Conrad's original intention, before he eventually developed the more complex idea of "The Secret Sharer", was to contrast the moral attitude of the English captain, with his inborn sense of comradeship and loyalty to the hunted man who has thrown himself on his mercy, with that of the selfish and unscrupulous Russian student, Razumov.

UNDER WESTERN EYES
AND
CRIME AND PUNISHMENT

Conrad never liked Dostoyevsky. After reading *The Brothers Karamazov,* he wrote to Edward Garnett, "Dostoyevsky is too Russian for me. It sounds to me like some fierce mouthing from prehistoric ages."*

But among Conrad scholars it is almost a commonplace to say that Conrad was influenced by Dostoyevsky. The matter requires examination.

The resemblances between *Under Western Eyes* and Dostoyevsky's *Crime and Punishment* are numerous indeed and cannot be considered accidental. In his basic *Joseph Conrad: A Critical Biography,* Jocelyn Baines observes: "There is a parallel between the course of events in *Under Western Eyes* and *Crime and Punishment.* Razumov and Raskolnikov commit an act, cowardly or criminal, which causes them mental agony and isolates them by destroying the possibility of normal relations with other human beings, and their torment finally drives them to confess."**

To these resemblances one may add love as a factor arousing the consciences of both, and leading them to confess their guilt: the strange illness of both after committing their crime: and the similar parts played by the driver Ziemianitch, in *Under Western Eyes,* and the house-painter in *Crime and Punishment,* both of whom are unjustly suspected and end by hanging themselves, thus diverting suspicion from the real culprits. The final situation in both books is much the same; the principal characters are freed from suspicion, that their confessions may be wholly voluntary.

---

* Garnett, *Letters from Joseph Conrad 1895-1924,* Indianapolis, 1928, p. 240.
** J. Baines, *Joseph Conrad,* London, 1960, p. 369.

This is not all. The drama of the two heroes is closely linked with the fate of a mother and sister (in Conrad's book the victim's, in Dostoyevsky's, the murderer's). Moreover, the sisters in the two books are strangely alike, both in appearance and character; and both mothers become, at the end, mentally deranged.

The acts of both men (and both are university students) are carefully thought out, and, from their own point of view, justified. Raskolnikov feels that, as an exceptional person, he has a right to kill; Razumov sees his betrayal of Haldin as a patriotic duty. Both regard themselves as superior to the rest of humanity, on whom they look down. And, almost to the end, neither admits his guilt.

In the conversations that the two men hold with other people, the subject of their crime comes up again and again, and both are on tenterhooks, fearing discovery. This continual anxiety makes them both suspicious and irritable, and therefore incomprehensible to their companions. Finally, there is an obvious likeness between the conversations, sinister in their apparent friendliness, between Mikulin and Razumov, and Raskolnikov and the judge Porphyry.

These are the most obvious resemblances. Others could be added, including many phrases in Conrad's novel, in which we catch echoes of *Crime and Punishment*. But enough has been said to exclude the possibility of an accidental likeness between the two books.

It seems obvious that *Under Western Eyes* is a more or less deliberate travesty of the theme of *Crime and Punishment*, although it might more justly be described as a parallel, but at the same time contrasting, presentation of a similar problem.

What led to this "re-writing" of Dostoyevsky's novel by Conrad? In one of his letters written to John Galsworthy while he was working on the book Conrad says: "I am trying to capture the very soul of things Russian". *Under Western Eyes* had behind it a profound and deliberate study of the Russian character and Russian problems, and Conrad undoubtedly drew on the unique material provided by Dostoyevsky. We should remember that Conrad's own experience of Russia was confined to memories of his childhood, and that he had to depend largely on the testimony of Russian writers, whose works he certainly read widely at this time. It is difficult to know whether the resemblances between these and his own novel about Russia were fully deliberate or not, but one thing seems certain — that he used *Crime and Punishment* as a source for his ideas and concepts, just as a writer may use material taken from real life. This has always been done, and the likenesses between Dostoyevsky's book and Conrad's have no more significance than has the utilisation in a work of art of actual facts taken from life.

In speaking of the possible influence of *Crime and Punishment*, we should differentiate between a genuine literary influence and the mere inclusion, in one work, of details found in another. The true influence of one writer on the imagination of another implies the existence, at least in part, of a similar ideology, atmosphere and emotional structure. But one could hardly conceive of two more different intellectual and emotional attitudes towards their subject and heroes than those of Dostoyevsky and Conrad in the novels under consideration. Dostoyevsky is so completely caught up in the atmosphere of his book that it seems like a nightmare of his own fevered brain; and Raskolnikov, criminal though he is, is also a tragic hero. In Conrad's book Russia is under the detached and at times ironic gaze of "Western Eyes", and the student Razumov appears as a lamentable figure which only the compassion of the author finally rescues from his contempt. There can be no question of Conrad's having borrowed the mood, moral judgement or emotional response of Dostoyevsky. One can only speak of an adoption, more or less conscious, of the bare elements of the plot.

Shakespeare himself was the supreme example of this kind of literary borrowing, for he helped himself freely to the material already used by other writers. But who would dare, in his case, to speak of influence?

In so far, then, as one can speak of the influence of Dostoyevsky's novel on Conrad's it can only be according to the definition of the Russian school of formalist criticism — an "influence of repudiation" — the influence that exists when the attitude of one writer calls forth a strong repulsive reaction in another, who, in consequence, opposes the original idea with his own entirely different concept. In such cases, the resemblances between the two situations are the instrument and indeed the condition, of a powerful opposition.

All this, however, does not fully explain Conrad's ability to penetrate so far into the labyrinth of "things Russian" in *Under Western Eyes*. Were the novels of Dostoyevsky and the other great Russian writers really capable of giving him such deep understanding of the Russian soul? It seems unlikely, and we should look elsewhere for a fuller explanation.

In a letter to Charles Chassé (June 31st 1924), Conrad wrote: "The critics detected in me a new note, and as, just when I began to write, they had discovered the existence of the Russian authors, they stuck that label on me under the name of Slavonism. What I venture to say is that it would have been more just to charge me, at most, with Polonism. The Polish temperament is, at any rate, far removed from Byzantine and Asiatic associations."

Conrad stressed this point more than once, firmly dissociating himself from the "Slav label". Nevertheless, one can trace Slav affinities, especially in his early writings. For instance, the indolent dreamer, Almayer — to speak only of Conrad's first novel — would fit very well into a Russian story about a man whose life ends in frustration and decay ("bylyi chelaviek").

Although, for nearly a thousand years, the Polish character has been moulded into the Western pattern by the Catholic Church and Poland's historic links with the West, the Poles are Slavs by origin and combine the features of Western and Eastern Europe. This is particularly true of those who, like Conrad, come from Eastern Poland.

Conrad, however, spent the whole of his adult life in England, a fact which must have affected, in favour of the West, the balance of Eastern and Western elements in his nature. But enough of the Slav still remained in his personality to give him a deep insight into the Russian people and Russian problems. On the other hand, his mind had become so deeply influenced by Western ways of thought that he was able to look from an emotional distance at Russian problems, and judge them quite impartially. It is largely this objectivity that makes *Under Western Eyes* such a great novel — a rival and a challenge to Dostoyevsky's masterpiece.

PART IV

THE AGEING CONRAD

FROM ACHIEVEMENT
TO DECLINE

Most Conrad scholars share the view that his writings can be divided into two distinct periods, differing widely in content and literary merit. Most of his best work was done when he was comparatively young, and it is on these earlier achievements that his fame now chiefly rests. His later work is marked by few original departures, and of artistic freshness there is little evidence, although the status of some of the works of this period remains controversial.

The dividing line would seem to fall somewhere between the completion of *Under Western Eyes* (1910) and the initial work done on *Chance*. There are, of course, some overlapping cases which do not conform to this pattern. *The Shadow Line*, for instance, and, up to a point, *Victory*, provide notable exceptions.

In general, however, the proposition seems to hold. Writing in depth, and penetrating psychological insights, are features mostly met with in the earlier work. In the later period, less original structures predominate. Even *Victory*, the most ambitious book of its period, is somewhat forced and artificial in style and structure; and *The Arrow of Gold* is admittedly a failure.

The obvious decline in the creative powers of a writer of Conrad's stature — a phenomenon which Hewitt and Moser were the first of Conrad's critics to point out — undoubtedly calls for analysis and explanation. Much comment has already been forthcoming, as well as some laboured solutions to the problem, such as the hypothesis put forward by Dr. Meyer in his *Psychological Biography of Conrad*, where he attributes the decline of the writer's powers to an alleged psychosis in 1910.

It is, however, rather surprising that such unusual — indeed, sensational — causes have been suggested when one very simple and natural explanation has been generally overlooked — an explanation which, if it did not account for everything, must have been at least an important factor.

As a doctor of medicine I myself find the deterioration in Conrad's powers explained, to a great extent, by purely physical factors — i.e. by the premature onset of old age.

Conrad apparently crossed his own "shadow line" in his early fifties. Certainly, as regards his appearance, he looked, in the photographs taken at that time, like an elderly man. There are writers who retain their creative powers much longer; but in Conrad's case, the ageing process started relatively early, and affected him both as a man and a writer.

He had suffered many hardships in his first forty years; his nervous system was unusually sensitive, and he was not physically strong. His life at sea, rough and tiring though it was, may have hardened and toughened him, but before he was forty he exchanged it for a literary career. The life he then led — working mostly at night, chain-smoking, and drinking innumerable cups of strong tea — could hardly have had a more ruinous effect on his health. And, on top of this, there were financial worries and the exhausting process of creative writing (every major book cost him an illness) to strain his nerves almost to breaking point.

Worse than all else, however, were his many illnesses, which towards the end of his life became much more frequent. Malaria played havoc with him and made him virtually an invalid; he had crippling arthritis and bad teeth, which he refused to have extracted. In fact, as was already suspected in his lifetime, a dental infection may have led indirectly to his severe arthritis and heart-trouble.

In 1910 he suffered from an unspecified but very serious illness (the starting-point of Dr. Meyer's hypothesis). This illness, as Jessie Conrad tells us, almost killed him, and may have done lasting damage to an organism past its youth. It could also have speeded up the normal advance of sclerosis, as often happens after a major disease in old age.

It seems certain that he died of a heart attack brought on by sclerosis of the coronary vessels. Generalised sclerosis had clearly been making rapid progress in him, causing the blood vessels of the brain to harden — a process that must have lessened his creative

*Conrad listening
to music.
    Drawing by M. Bone.*

*Conrad reading.
    Drawing by M. Bone.*

183

ability. In view of all this, we may well marvel that he was able, towards the end of his life, to produce such a little masterpiece as *The Rover.**

In Conrad's later work, with which we are here concerned, we can distinguish four main characteristics: first the stiffening of his moral attitude, as represented by the Lingard type of hero; secondly the abandonment of psychological analysis, of passionate probing into the riddle of life and human character — in favour of romantic dreaming and an interest in the dramatic rather than the philosophical and psychological aspects of man's destiny; a gradual withdrawal into the region of past reminiscences; and, finally, a certain rigidity — even at times clumsiness — of artistic expression.

It is easy to see that these are not exceptional but typical manifestations of advancing age. People as they grow older usually turn into stricter moralists; they tend to escape from surrounding reality into the realm of memories; and they become, as they were in early youth, more interested in the dramatic and romantic than in the psychological aspects of man's life. There occurs also, as a rule, a weakening of mental powers. In writers it is the creative powers which are first affected.

In Conrad these characteristics were even more comprehensible than they usually are in ageing authors. His fidelity to ethical principle, and his romantic love of adventure and heroism, even when these verge on melodrama, appeared in his books right from the beginning. (We need only recall "Youth" and *Romance*). What could be more natural than that these elements should become intensified and almost dominate his work at a time of life when most authors are drawn to precisely this kind of writing?

As regards the last element — intellectual decline — Conrad managed to escape it quite successfully. Although no longer the

---

* A. J. Guérard, one of the critics who stressed the sudden decline in Conrad's creative power, sees, as I do, simple and natural reasons for its occurrence after 1910. He writes in his book *Conrad the Novelist*: "One reason for the imaginative decline is not obscure at all: physical and mental fatigue." He also points very convincingly to the causes of this fatigue: the exhaustion that must have followed on Conrad's astounding creative effort between 1894 and 1910.

To this I would add that the theory of Conrad's exhaustion having been caused by volcanic explosion of creative power is the more convincing in that this "explosion" took place in his later life and poured out in one great torrent all that had been accumulating within him during his years at sea. After this tremendous effort there was not much left — particularly as no dramatic experience came his way from the stabilised life of a writer. This also accounts for his swift "burning-out".

consummate artist he once was, his mind remained perfectly lucid and alert to the very end; some of his clearest intellectual formulations belong to this period. The fact that most of them are stereotypes, and that he no longer made any fresh discoveries, need not surprise us, and we should not ask for more than he gave us.

It is an attribute of man in his prime to discover and hoard truths about life and people; in old age even the liveliest mind can only use and perfect the material it has already amassed.

All this is fairly obvious, but I think it was worth pointing out, for such things are easily forgotten in any discussion of the psycho-literary decline of Conrad's creative powers. Although a few Conrad scholars (Moser, and Guerard whom I have already quoted) took the question of Conrad's physical health into account, it was only as a contributing factor, whereas, in my opinion, it was fundamental and decisive. Simple solutions, as we know, are often the last to be considered, for they are less spectacular and attractive than the more sophisticated alternatives.

WAS THE AGEING CONRAD
SINCERE IN HIS MORAL BELIEFS?

There is a tendency today to regard Conrad's later work as being not only inferior from the literary point of view but superficial and insincere in its approach to the fundamental problems of our existence. To quote D. Hewitt, the precursor of this trend (*Conrad: A Reassessment*, London, 1969; first published in 1952): "The lush and imprecise rhetoric and the portentous and equally imprecise moralising... which are predominant features of *Chance* and *Victory* and *The Rover* and *The Arrow of Gold*, are signs of uneasiness and evasion, of an inability to sustain the tension set up by that awareness of corruption and loneliness which gives such force to his best work."*

Critics who hold the view that Conrad's greatness lay in the nature and expression of his scepticism — his questioning of every recognised human value, behind which he saw yawning an abyss of corruption and evil — appreciate and admire only the writer's first creative period, which they see dominated by his pessimism and moral despair; they believe that in his later books, which tend rather to affirm moral values, Conrad betrayed his inner convictions and shut his eyes to the bitter truth.

Believing as I do that this trend of thinking is founded on a misapprehension, I propose to challenge it.

Such criticism seems to me a striking example of intellectual daltonism, which allows those affected by it to see only certain aspects of a given question, while blinding them to others equally essential. The admirers of Conrad the pessimist are so intent on their concept of the "real" Conrad — a Conrad who is essentially "nihilistic" — that they do not see or cannot fully realise that both

---

* Hewitt, p. 117.

Conrad in Zakopane in 1914.

attitudes — the sceptical and the affirmative — appear, in varying proportions, all through his creative life: and that both bear the same unmistakable imprint of deep sincerity. Such critics ignore the obvious fact that *Heart of Darkness, Lord Jim* and *Typhoon* contain in embryo the same principles that were later embodied in Conrad's system of "a very few simple ideas" on which, according to him, the whole world rests; and that the moral code, to them so distasteful, of his later period, can be traced back to the earlier work that they most admire. In their view, it is not the conflict but the note of moral despair in Conrad — Conrad the pessimist, not Conrad the fighter — that alone holds any interest or value.

The one-sidedness of this attitude makes it impossible for these critics to see Conrad as a whole — to listen with the same attentiveness and objectivity to the two voices within him, engaged in a continual dialogue between the intellectual scepticism that questions all human values, and the upright and independent character that will not abandon these values. The chief defect of this way of thinking lies, not in the refusal to appreciate the other — the positive — side of Conrad, but in the inability to believe in its sincerity — the suspicion that it was only self-deception, a cover-up for Conrad's moral doubt.

In this supposed insincerity the modern school of criticism also sees the cause of Conrad's decline as a writer during the second phase of his literary career. One is, of course, bound to agree that in his later work Conrad is no more the consummate artist he was. It is also true that in these books he no longer pursues his quest for the meaning of life, but turns from its disturbing problems to extol a few simple moral principles; and that this change of direction restricts his field and robs his imagination of some of its riches. But there is no justification for seeing in this change the only reason for his diminished power as an artist (there were other reasons, discussed by me in the previous chapter), or for accusing him of being unable to face reality and being untrue to himself. On the contrary, it is my strong belief that up to the very end Conrad never lacked the courage to look into the depths of himself and form a true judgement of what he saw there.

I myself know something of these matters, and — *toutes proportions gardées* — speak from my own experience. I too, being old, have ceased to gaze into depths which I know I can never fathom — ceased, not out of fear, or the refusal to face reality, but because I know I cannot go beyond what I have already seen, and because at present the matter does not seem to me of the first importance. I do not think I am being cowardly or disloyal to my former self in deliberately adopting my present position. I also feel that I am now able to see more clearly — more from within myself — into the truth of Conrad's later life, and that I am therefore entitled to speak of it.

To sum up this short analysis: those who accept and admire Conrad the sceptic, but who dismiss him as a moralist, not only distort the picture of the world that Conrad gave us, but deprive it of an essential and most important element. For what made him a great and outstanding figure was precisely the combination, the very rare combination, of pessimism with defiance — of profound scepticism with that human pride which will never wholly submit to doubt and helpless despair.

Conrad with his cousin in 1924.

BIBLIOGRAPHY

(This bibliography gives only a selection of the books published on the subject)

Conrad's Works; Letters from and to Conrad

Collected Edition of the Works of Joseph Conrad, J. M. Dent and Sons Ltd., 1946-55.
Sisters, New York 1928 — Milan 1968.
Conrad's Prefaces, with an Introductory Essay by Edward Garnett, London, 1937.
The Life and Letters of Joseph Conrad, edited by G. Jean-Aubry, London, 1927.
Joseph Conrad's Letters to His Wife, with a Preface by Jessie Conrad, London, 1927.
Letters from Conrad 1895-1924, with an Introduction by Edward Garnett, London, 1928.
Conrad to a Friend: 150 letters from Joseph Conrad to Richard Curle, London, 1928.
Letters to William Blackwood and David S. Meldrum, Durham. N. C., 1958.
Conrad's Polish Background: Letters to and from Polish Friends edited by Z. Najder, Oxford, 1964.
Lettres Françaises, ed. G. Jean-Aubry, Paris, 1930.
Lettres de Joseph Conrad à Marguerite Poradowska, ed. René Rapin, Genève, 1966.
Joseph Conrad: Listy, oprac. Z. Najder, Warszawa, 1968.
Bobrowski Tadeusz, *Listy do Conrada*, oprac. R. Jabłkowska, Warszawa, 1981.

Bibliographical Studies

Grzegorczyk P., *Joseph Conrad w Polsce*, Warszawa, 1933.
Lohf K. A. and E. P. Sheehy, *Joseph Conrad at Mid-Century 1895-1955*, Minneapolis, 1957.
Ehrsam T. G., *A Bibliography of Joseph Conrad*, Methuen, N.Y., 1969.
Teets Bruce, and Helmut Gerber, *Joseph Conrad: An Annotated Bibliography of Writings about Him*, De Kalb, Illinois, 1971.

Biographies and Memoirs

Baines J., *Joseph Conrad: A Critical Biography*, London, 1960.
Bobrowski T., *Pamiętniki*, Lwów, 1900.
Braun A., *Śladami Conrada*, Warszawa, 1972.
Buszczyński S., *Malo znany poeta*, Kraków, 1970.

Conrad Borys, *My Father: Joseph Conrad*, London, 1970.
Conrad Jessie, *Joseph Conrad as I Knew Him*, London, 1926.
  Joseph Conrad and His Circle, London, 1935.
Conrad John, *Joseph Conrad: Times Remembered*, Cambridge, 1981.
Curle R., *The Last Twelve Years of Joseph Conrad*, London, 1928.
Ford M. Ford (Hueffer), *Joseph Conrad, a Personal Remembrance*, London, 1924.
  Return to Yesterday, London, 1931.
Fredro A., *Trzy po trzy*, Warszawa, 1957
Galsworthy J., *Castles in Spain*, London, 1927.
Jean-Aubry G., *Vie de Conrad*, Paris, 1947.
Karl F. R., *Joseph Conrad: The Three Lives, A Biography*, London, 1979.
Megroz R. L., *A Talk with Joseph Conrad*, London, 1926.
Najder Z., *Ludzie żywi: Życie Conrada Korzeniowskiego*, 2 vols., Warszawa, 1980.
Retinger J. H., *Conrad and His Contemporaries*, London, 1941.
Russell B., *Portraits from Memory*, 1956.
Watt I., *Conrad in the Nineteenth Century*, London, 1980.

Criticism

Bradbrook M. C., *Joseph Conrad; Poland's English Genius*, Cambridge, 1941.
Busza A., *Conrad's Polish Literary Background*, Roma, 1966.
Curle R., *Joseph Conrad; a Study*, London, 1914.
Crankshaw J., *Joseph Conrad; Some Aspects of the Art of Novel*, London, 1936.
Dąbrowska M., *Szkice o Conradzie*, Warszawa, 1959.
Fleishman Avrom, *Conrad's Politics*, Baltimore, 1967.
Forster E. M., *Abinger Harvest*, London, 1936.
Gillon A., *The Eternal Solitary*, New York, 1960.
Gordan J. D., *The Making of a Novelist*, Cambridge, Mass., 1940.
Grabowski Z., *Ze studiów nad J. Conradem*, Poznań, 1927.
Guerard A. J., *Conrad the Novelist*, Cambridge, Mass., 1958.
Hay E. Knapp, *The Political Novels of Joseph Conrad*, Chicago, 1963.
Hewitt D., *Conrad; A Reassessment*, Cambridge, 1952.
Hodges R. R., *The Dual Heritage of Joseph Conrad*, The Hague, 1967.
  Hommage à Joseph Conrad, NRF, Paris, 1924.
Howe I., *Politics and the Novel*, New York, 1957.
Jabłkowska R., *Joseph Conrad Korzeniowski*, Warszawa, 1964.
Kirschner P., *Conrad: the Psychologist as Artist*, Edinburgh, 1968.
Kocówna B. (ed.) *Wspomnienia i studia o Conradzie*, Warszawa, 1963.
  Polskość Conrada, Kraków, 1967.
Komar M., *Piekło Conrada*, Warszawa, 1978.
Krzyżanowski L. (ed.), *Joseph Conrad: Centennial Essays*, New York, 1960.
Leavis F. R., *The Great Tradition*, London, 1948.
Mann T., *Past Masters and Other Papers*, London, 1933.
Mencken H., *Book of Prefaces*, London, 1922.

192

Meyer B. C., *Joseph Conrad; a Psychoanalytic Biography*, Princeton, U.S.A., 1967.

Morf G., *The Polish Heritage of Joseph Conrad*, London, 1930.

The Polish Shades and Ghosts of Joseph Conrad, New York, 1976.

Moser T., *Joseph Conrad; Achievement and Decline*, Cambridge, Mass., 1957.

Mroczkowski P., *Conradian Commentaries*, Kraków, 1970.

Najder Z., *Nad Conradem*, Warszawa, 1965.

Palmer J. A., *Joseph Conrad's Fiction*, Cornell University Press, 1968.

Sherry N., *Conrad's Eastern World*, Cambridge, 1966.

Conrad's Western World, Cambridge, 1971.

Stallman R. W. (ed.) *The Art of Joseph Conrad; a Critical Symposium*, Michigan, 1960.

Symons A., *Notes on Joseph Conrad*, London, 1925.

Tarnawski W. (ed.), *Conrad Żywy*, London, 1957.

Conrad, Człowiek — Pisarz — Polak, Londyn, 1972.

Ujejski J., *Joseph Conrad*, Traduit par P. Duméril, 1939. (French translation of *O Konradzie Korzeniowskim*, Warszawa, 1936).

Walpole H., *Joseph Conrad*, London, 1916.

Warner O., *Joseph Conrad*, London, 1951.

Watts C. T., *A Preface to Conrad*, (Preface books), London and New York, 1982.

Woolf V., *The Common Reader*, London, 1925.

Zabierowski S., *Conrad w Polsce*, Gdańsk, 1971.

Żeromski S., *Joseph Conrad, Pisma wybrane*, (Introduction to the selected edition of Conrad's Works). Warszawa, 1923.

INDEX

The quotations from Conrad's writings are taken from the **Collected Edition of the Works of Joseph Conrad, J**. M. Dent and Sons Ltd., 1946-55, London.

1 index

195

heroism, 82; isolation, 60, 62, 164; loneliness, 31, 32, 44, 130; loyalty, 94, 104, 111, 142; material interests, 68, 156, 164; romanticism, 72, 84, 85, 86, 106, 107, 135; youth, 82, 85, 86, 106, 107, 135.
Cornelius, (character), 73

4 index